DIRECTING THE HEART

Weekly Mindfulness Teachings and Practices from the Torah

By Rabbi Yael Levy

A Way In
Philadelphia, Pennsylvania
awayin.org

Also by Rabbi Yael Levy

Journey through the Wilderness:
A Mindfulness Approach to the Ancient Jewish Practice of Counting the Omer

Published by:
A Way In
Philadelphia, Pennsylvania
awayin.org

Paperback ISBN 978-1-7332384-0-3

Library of Congress Control Number: 2019912029

Design by Amy Pollack, Twistnshout

Introduction

One thing we know for certain: Life is in constant motion. Everything is always changing.

As life unfolds, we create relationships, form connections and become attached to people, places and experiences. Because everything passes, because we are each here for a limited time, we are always letting go.

Holding on and letting go: a mysterious and challenging paradox of existence. Family, friendships, community, and relationships are the treasures of life, bringing us meaning, joy and gratitude.

Yet the stronger our relationships, the deeper our connections, the more sadness and pain we feel at the letting go. The more we love, the deeper our bonds, the more wrenching the inevitable losses.

How do we live fully with the awareness that life will end?
How do we love continuously even as we experience loss?
How do we embrace joy, gratitude and beauty?
How do we live with disappointments, sadness and pain?
To be human is to ask these questions.

The rituals, traditions and sacred texts of Judaism help me find meaning in the complexities and contradictions of life. They encourage my gratitude and joy and help me navigate pain and disappointment. They support me well as I experience the truth of impermanence.

In Deuteronomy (6: 4-9), we hear Judaism's central call, *Shema Yisrael:* Listen, Israel, and then *Ve'ahafta:* And you will love.

Listen and you will love. Pay Attention. Be mindful as you sit in your house and as you walk on your way. Pay attention, listen, as you rest and as you go forth.

Notice, be aware of your words, actions and responses and you will develop the capacity to meet with love whatever life brings.

Shema . . . Ve'ahafta. Listen and you will learn to love. This teaching puts mindfulness practice at the heart of Jewish tradition. It helps us notice that the tradition is filled with practices that call forth our awareness and attention.

Many times a day, the tradition urges us to notice, to pay attention, to be mindful. Through the practice of saying blessings, we are called to pause in wonder, to give thanks for nourishment, to notice trees, gaze at the ocean, look up at the sky. Through prayer and ritual, the tradition calls us to embrace joy and be present with sadness and loss.

And once every week, on Shabbat, we are called to step out of the busyness of our lives, to stop reaching, striving, and creating. Once each week, we take time to return our awareness to our interdependent relationship with the natural world. Shabbat calls us to stop doing and practice being.

Shema, Ve'ahafta: Listen, pause, pay attention and we will cultivate the capacity to respond to life's experiences with wisdom and compassion.

It is through the prism of this central call that I have explored each portion in the five books of the Torah, listening for wisdom to help us live mindfully and navigate well this paradoxical and mysterious gift of life. Many teachings are gleaned from a small piece of text that touched my heart and opened my awareness in a new way. These texts, I believe, direct the heart and focus our attention, strengthening our ability to meet well all we encounter. The English translations of the Biblical Hebrew offered here are mine. Some are direct translations; others are more interpretative. I pray that what I have heard honors the text.

The offerings in this book grew out of an online series I wrote a few years ago for the Institute for Jewish Spirituality, an organization that has been central in my learning and development. The Institute trains rabbis and other Jewish leaders in mindfulness practice with the goal of revitalizing and expanding Jewish life. I am so grateful for the guidance and wisdom they continue to offer.

My hope is that the teachings in this book inspire courage and love and, in the words of the psalmist, guide us to:

Trust in the unfolding of life,
Act for good, and meet well whatever life brings.   *Psalm 37:3*

Rabbi Yael Levy
December 31, 2018
23 Tevet 5779

How to Use this Book

This book is arranged according to the cycle of reading the Torah, the Five Books of Moses, that begins each year in the fall. The exact beginning date fluctuates depending upon the *Yamim Noraim*, the Jewish High Holy Days, but the order of the readings is always the same. As the Holidays come to an end, we join the end of the Torah to the beginning and start the cycle again. During the year, as we travel through the seasons, we make our way through each of the five books.

This book provides teachings and mindfulness practices for each Torah portion, inspired by a verse, idea, or a story in the text.

There are many ways to use this book in your own practice.

You could follow the Jewish cycle of the Torah and read each section aligned with the Jewish calendar, beginning the book and your practice where we are in the Jewish year cycle.

You could start the book at the beginning and follow it all the way through week by week, no matter where we are in the Jewish calendar.

You can have a practice that invites you to open up the book at random and notice what teachings you find.

However you begin, I suggest you explore these teachings with a weekly practice, focusing on one teaching/practice each week.

These teachings are designed to stand on their own, but placing the verses in context by reading some or part of the original Torah text might enhance your experience.

At the beginning of each week, I recommend reading the teaching once or twice on your own or with a study partner.

Even if you are on your own, I encourage you to read the teaching aloud. Forming the words and hearing them invites us into a different relationship with the material. Afterward, read the suggested practice and set aside time each day for meditation.

A practice is strengthened through repetition and consistency. If possible, set aside a similar time each day for the meditation practice.

It is important, as we begin, to take on practices that are realistic. Most of the practices in this book invite us to meditate for 5, 10 or 15 minutes each day. If you already have a practice, you might want to sit for a longer time. Or perhaps you might want to sit for 5-15 minutes for the first few weeks and then lengthen the sits after some time. Sitting for 5, 10 or 15 minutes each day is a substantial practice that will bring forth much benefit.

It could also be that taking on a daily practice is not realistic and you might want to make a commitment to sit 2-4 times a week instead of every day.

Practice requires discipline and compassion. Discipline helps us break through resistance and do the practice even when we don't feel like it. Compassion offers forgiveness when we don't fulfill all we had expected and can help us recommit without having to feel bad about ourselves. And the balance between discipline and compassion is a constant dance—a practice in and of itself.

It takes time to develop a practice and the more we do it the stronger the practice muscles become. After a while of reaching for the practice, we will begin to feel it calling to us. It will become something our systems are used to and begin to yearn for.

There will be teachings and practices in the book that touch you more than others, and there could be some that don't touch you at all. Sometimes it might be good to make modifications to the suggested practices. Other times it will feel wise to do the practice anyway and be with the discomfort. And sometimes it might be the right thing not to do certain practices that really do not feel true. When exploring these possibilities, it is always good to sit with the question: What is the wise and compassionate choice?

And then do our best to wait patiently for an answer.

During the week, you might want to write in a journal, noting responses to the teachings and practices and recording insights that arise for you.

This book is meant to be of service. I hope it can help create and strengthen regular practice and reveal teachings that expand our perspectives, encourage our awareness, and inspire compassionate and generous actions.

Torah Portions

Beresheet
The Book of Genesis

Shemot
The Book of Exodus

Vayikra
The Book of Leviticus

B'midbar
The Book of Numbers

D'varim
The Book of Deuteronomy

Beresheet
The Book of Genesis

Beresheet: Beginnings

Light spilled out of darkness.
Waters rose and were gathered.
Land formed and vegetation came forth.
Orbs of light glowed in the expanse of sky.
Living beings emerged
And started to crawl, swim, fly.
And then from the *adamah*, from the dust of the earth, *Adam* was formed,
A vessel sculpted out of clay.
Into this vessel, the Eternal blew *neshmat chayim*, the breath of life,
And humankind came to be.

And here we are — *nefesh chayah*, living beings.

The first people, *Adam* and *Chavah* (whose names mean earth and life),
Were placed in a magnificent world,
A garden of perfection.

Streams of connection flowed freely.
Beauty was everywhere.

Adam and *Chavah* were placed in this world
With the freedom to make choices.
And *Adam* and *Chavah* chose to eat
from *aytz hada'at tov v'rah*,
The Tree of the Knowledge of Good and Evil.
They choose to live with *tov v'rah*, the good and bad,
Paradox and contradiction.
They chose to know the fullness of life
And the experience of death.

Once they ate from this tree,
Adam and *Chavah* knew
That life is impermanent.
Everything would come forth
And eventually pass.
They themselves would live, love,
Work, struggle, flourish
And die.

The world of creation, they now knew,
Was filled with abundant blessings
And deep sadness and pain
And would unfold within a mystery
They could never control or fully understand.
And this knowledge made them afraid,
So they clothed themselves for protection.

The spirit of God,
The spirit of the Mystery,
Blew through the garden
And formed a question,
The very first question ever put to human beings:
Ayekah? Where are you?   *Genesis 3:9*
When *Adam* and *Chavah* heard this question, they hid.

And the question continued to go forth:
Ayekah? Where are you?

Finally, *Adam* and *Chavah* answered.
We heard your voice.
We knew you were with us in the garden
But we were afraid.   *Genesis 3:10*

    We were afraid because we were naked.
    We were ashamed because we were vulnerable.
    We were overwhelmed
    Because we saw the complexity of life
    And the certainty of death,
    So we hid.

Ayekah? Where are you?
The question continues to call in each moment.
Ayekah? Where are you?
Who at times does not want to hide?
Who at times does not feel afraid, ashamed, vulnerable?
Who at times does not feel overwhelmed
By the complexities, paradoxes and challenges of life?

Our creation story acknowledges that wanting to hide
Is a natural tendency and at times a reasonable response

To the challenges of life.
And the Torah calls us to reach for a different response,
To hear the call *Ayekah*, Where are you?
And cultivate the capacity to respond:
Hineni, Here I am.

Hineni, Here I am, present in this very moment.
Hineni, Here I am, open to whatever this moment asks of me.
Here I am, willing to be in whatever is true.
Hineni, Here I am.

PRACTICE FOR THE WEEK
Sitting with the Question *Ayekah* and Responding *Hineni*

We begin by taking our seats and bringing ourselves to an awake and upright posture.

Bringing our attention to the breath, we begin to hear the call *Ayekah? Where are you?*
After a few calm, even, deep breaths, we respond, *Hineni, Here I am.*
We continue to repeat this phrase, letting it travel on the breath, feeling it move through the body. *Hineni, Here I am.*

When we notice that our attention has wandered, (as it will again and again), we gently bring ourselves back to the moment by saying, *Hineni, Here I am.*

At the close of the sit, we give thanks for the practice of returning to the present moment and we set an intention to pause three times during the day and say *Hineni, Here I am.*

Noach: Noah

Creation had gone awry.
The world had become corrupt.
Greed, contempt and a complete disregard of others
Had become the mode of being.

But Noah found favor in God's sight,
And he was chosen to build *a teva,* an ark,
That would withstand the destruction
That God was planning.

Into the ark, Noah was told to bring his family
And representatives of all the birds, animals,
And creatures that walked upon the earth.

Noah responded to God's directive
With silence.
He asked no questions.
He posed no arguments.
He built the ark,
Gathered his family and the animals,
And then watched as the flood
Destroyed all the living things that were upon the earth.

Noah was a righteous man within his generation.
Noah walked with God. *Genesis 6:9*

Perhaps Noah was chosen, not for who he was
But for who he could become.

Make a tzohar *in the ark, God instructed,* *Genesis 6:16*
An opening for something new to come through.

And in the ark, something new did come through.
Noah changed.
Responsible for the well-being of living creatures,
Something shifted deep inside.
Noah became alert, attentive, kind.
He rediscovered curiosity.

He grew interested in the diversity of creation.
And, as his awareness of the interconnection of all life grew,
Sensitivity, compassion
And a deep abiding care for others emerged.
And with this turning the world was renewed.

Creation unfolds in mystery
And everything we do matters.
By caring for each other,
For the animals, birds and all the earth,
We create a *tzohar*, an opening,
For kindness, love, and awareness
To shine through.
And with this
The world is renewed.

PRACTICE FOR THE WEEK

Blessing Practice

Even with the best of intentions, it can be easy to let harsh
judgments, impatience and disregard for others shape our words
and actions. This week, we practice cultivating compassion and
strengthening our capacity to return again and again to alert,
attentive kindness and care.

We begin by taking our seats and bringing attention to the breath,
noticing how the body moves to receive a breath and how it moves
to release a breath.

After a few moments, we draw our attention to the heart space,
noticing the breath fill the chest and torso. With gentle kindness,
we place upon our hearts the intention to send blessings into the
world.

We begin by turning toward ourselves and offering this prayer:

May I be blessed with love,
May I be blessed with peace,

May I be blessed with well-being.

We then call to our attention someone we love fully and easily and we say to this person:

May you be blessed with love,
May you be blessed with peace,
May you be blessed with well-being.

We then call to awareness someone we expect to encounter today and we say to this person:

May you be blessed with love,
May you be blessed with peace,
May you be blessed with well-being.

Lech Lecha: Go Forth

Lech Lecha, Go.
Leave what you know.
Leave who you have been.
Leave the old habits and ways
That have defined and shaped your life.

Take your strength, your support and what inspires your love
And go.

The destination is unknown,
But as you travel the path will appear.

And the goal of the journey?

The reason to leap,
To risk, to let go,
Is to be a blessing,
To discover anew the good that you are
And the many ways the Divine can come through you into the world.

It is difficult to leave, to let go and begin
And we are called to make this journey again and again.
There will be challenges along the way,
Heartache and pain.
We will make mistakes,
We will rise,
We will fall,
And we will rise again.

Messengers will guide us.
Gifts will appear.

And even as fear arises
And doubts assail,
Let us not be deterred,
Because the ways we journey through this life matters,
Not just for us
But for all those who will call us ancestor.

The path awaits our willingness.
The world awaits our blessings.
Let us go.

PRACTICE FOR THE WEEK

On the Journey

We take our seats with awareness, bringing ourselves to an awake and upright posture and let the attention rest on the breath.

As we begin the sit, we acknowledge that we are always being called forth into the fullness of our lives. Sometimes the call is welcome and brings great joy and other times the call is challenging and filled with doubt and fear.

On all our paths and in all our ways, the psalmist urges us to affirm: *This I know, the Infinite Presence is with me.*   *Psalm 56:10*

As I journey, as I struggle and fall, as I rise up and leap, as I get lost and as I find my way: *This I know, the Infinite Presence is with me.*

We sit with this verse, repeating it over and over, letting it travel on our breath and fill our bodies. We do our best not to attach a story to the verse and every time we notice our attention has wandered, we bring ourselves gently back to the breath and to the Psalmist's call: *This I know, the Infinite Presence is with me.*

At the close of the sit, we set an intention to notice messengers that help guide our way.

Vayera: The Mystery Appeared

Abraham sat at the opening of his tent and God appeared.
Lifting his eyes, Abraham saw God in three men who walked across
the desert.
He saw God in the promise of a longed-for birth
And in the contention that followed.
He saw God in the striving for justice
And in devastation and destruction.
He saw God in pain and sorrow.
He saw God in all that he loved and all that he sacrificed.

Abraham lifted his eyes and saw the paradox and contradictions of life.
He saw the tugging of bonds and allegiances.
He saw the struggle for peace
And the wreckage of violence.
He saw the pain of loving.

Abraham sat at the opening of his tent in the heat of the day
And God appeared.
All life swirled by —
A tangled, messy web of experience
That asks of us
Everything.
And Abraham named this place of knowing *Adonai yireh*, God sees.

Each new day we sit at the opening.
    What will appear?
    What will be asked of us?
    What will we notice, long for, seek?
    How will we meet each encounter?

Abraham sat at the opening of his tent in the heat of the day.
God appeared and Abraham lifted his eyes.
Abraham recognized God in the promises
And disappointments of life
And he rose to greet this awareness.

PRACTICE FOR THE WEEK

Sitting at the Opening, Lifting our Eyes

We make a commitment to sit at the opening of each moment and place upon our hearts the intention to notice whatever arises with non-judgmental awareness, to greet each thought, each feeling, as a visitor that is passing through.

Sitting in an awake and upright posture, letting our attention rest on the breath, we notice the sensations of receiving a breath and the sensations of releasing a breath. As the mind drifts to thoughts, we practice noticing whatever arises and letting each thought, each story pass by. We say to ourselves: The mind is thinking, telling stories, posing questions or challenges. The mind is bringing forth feelings, fears, hopes or dreams.

Then we return our attention to the breath. The goal is not to stop our thoughts, but rather to practice greeting each thought without judgment or fear.

When we begin to constrict around a feeling or when we become aware of following a story, we return to the moment by acknowledging the thought, feeling, sensation and return our attention to the breath over and over again.

We close the sit by giving thanks for the opportunity to sit at the opening and greet whatever arises.

Chayei Sarah: The Life of Sarah

Moments pass,
Days become years,
Life begins and ends.

In this there is no choice.

But every day, in every encounter, we make decisions:
    Where we will offer our most precious gifts —
        Our time,
        Our love,
        Our devotion.

Sarah's life had come to an end and Abraham realized it was time for
Isaac to be married. He sent his servant to find the right woman in the
land that he and Sarah had left.

The servant journeyed and prayed. He prayed for the ability to fulfill his
mission and he asked to find and to receive *chesed* – kindness, love and
generosity. When he arrived at the village he was seeking, he placed these
prayers upon his heart.

And as he did, Rebecca appeared, walking down to the spring.
As she came up from the well, she saw the man who had been praying.
I will draw water for you and your camels until they finish drinking,
she offered.   Genesis 24:19

To provide water for a man and camels who have journeyed across the
desert, Rebecca needed to go down to the well many times. Yet her
offerings seemed effortless and unattached to reward or expectation.

What does it take to go down to the well,
To find the spring, the source,
To come up and share our offerings?
And then to go back down to the well again and again,
Filling our vessels with living waters,
Sharing our sustenance without hesitation,
Giving of ourselves with grace and love?

It is so easy to get stuck in webs of mistrust and fear,
The briars, the thickets of thoughts and stories that insist
We can't,
We shouldn't,
We aren't enough.

Go down to the well, the portion calls,
Go deep and find what is yours to give.
And when rising up, be discerning.
Notice what offerings come from fullness
And what offerings rise from "shoulds" and "have-tos"
That are not kind or true.
Notice when the offerings result in depletion and disconnection
And when they inspire further generosity, honesty and love.

Moments pass,
Days become years.
This is our one life, right now.

Chesed — kindness, compassion, generosity —
Calls us down to the well,
Encourages us to reach deep
To discover our offerings
And then rise up full and able
To give our gifts with love.

PRACTICE FOR THE WEEK

Sitting with Prayer, Making Requests

We begin our sit by calling ourselves present: focusing on the
breath, letting our attention rest on the motion of the body as it
receives and releases a breath.

After a few minutes, we ask ourselves with kindness and interest:
What prayer is within me today?

What is a longing, a yearning I feel?
What is something I seek or hope?

We notice any resistance or judgments that might arise and do our best not to follow these thoughts. Again and again, we return to the breath and gently ask ourselves to find and articulate a prayer. When one arises, we repeat it to ourselves, letting it travel with the breath. We place the prayer upon our hearts. If a prayer does not arrive, we notice this with kindness and follow the breath with gentleness. We close the sit with the intention that our prayers will inspire our actions and help open the ways forward.

After the sit each day, we might want to write down the prayer we discovered.

Toldot: Generations

As Isaac's life unfolded,
He became a digger of wells.

First Isaac re-dug his father's wells.

He returned to the place his father had been.
He searched and uncovered the wells his father had found
And he gave them the same names his father had given them.
For Isaac, something old and something new was revealed.

Then Isaac began to dig his own wells.
He reached into the thick, dark earth.
He dug into deep and hidden places
And encountered the well where discord and strife reside,
Where needs, wants and desires clash,
And make it almost impossible
To see oneself or another,
A place so filled with pain and conflict
That lashing out seems to be the only possible response.

And Isaac named the well of this experience *Esek*: Contention.

Genesis 26:20

And Isaac kept digging.
Reaching deeper, he came to a well that was filled with fear,
That was overflowing with doubt,
A well where his greatest demons thrived
And he named this well, this experience, *Sitnah*: Demonic Fear.

Genesis 26:21

And Isaac kept digging.
He would not be turned away by contention.
He would not be stopped by fears.
He kept digging, reaching,
Until he found an opening
Where he could see beyond what frightened him
And caused so much of his struggle and pain.

Isaac kept exploring until he touched
A spacious perspective,
Wide enough to see possibilities
That could help him discern the best ways to move forward.
And he named the well of this experience *Rehovot:* Expanse.

Genesis 26:22

And here Isaac heard the Infinite call, *Do not be afraid. With you, I am.*

Genesis 26:24

Isaac stands at places of transition,
Guarding the passage, showing the way.
He says to himself and to us:
Dig deep.
Don't be waylaid by contention,
Don't be stopped by fear.
This is never all there is.
Keep searching. Keep looking. Keep returning.
There is a way into the expanse
And the journey is continuous.

We rise. We fall. We rise again.
We gain perspective and lose it.
We are besieged by doubt and fears.
We are released into the expanse of possibility.
The journey is continuous.

Reach deep, Isaac says,
And open to the presence of the Mystery.
For the Infinite calls,
Do not be afraid. Wherever you are, with you, I am.

PRACTICE FOR THE WEEK

Sitting in the Wells of Experience

As we sit this week, we make a commitment to be in the wells of our own experiences. We acknowledge and honor wherever we find ourselves. We make a commitment to meet ourselves with love and compassion.

We take our seats, bringing ourselves to an awake, upright posture and let the attention rest gently on the breath. As thoughts arise, we notice the sensations that the thoughts create in the body. We notice as thoughts create constriction and as they bring feelings of relaxation and calm.

When we become aware that the mind is following a thought or story away from the present moment, we give thanks for noticing and return our attention to the breath.

Toward the end of the sit, we invite ourselves to hear the Infinite's call to Isaac and to us — *Itcha Anochi* — With you, I am. We place this call upon our hearts, reminding ourselves that wherever we are, whatever we are feeling or experiencing, the Divine Presence is with us.

Vayetzei: Going Out

Jacob left all he had known,
All he had been,
And traveled into the dark.
Laying his head upon a rock,
He sought sleep.

But Jacob was startled awake.
He was awakened by the magnitude of the Divine Presence:
A vision of a ladder reaching from the earth to the heavens,
Angels ascending and descending,
And the Infinite, the Mystery of All Being,
Standing beside him.

Break through, the Infinite called to Jacob.   *Genesis 28:14*

> Break through your fears and assumptions.
> Break through who you have been
> And who you thought you should be.
> Break through the limits of your imagination,
> And awaken to the mysteries of life.
>
> Awaken to the complexities of truth.
> Awaken to who you are in your fullness
> And what is yours to do.
> Wake up and be present.
> Wake up and live.

Jacob trembled in fear.
He trembled at the magnitude of the call.
He shuddered at all he needed to let go of,
And all he needed to become.

The Holy One was in this place and I, I, did not know it,
Jacob whispered to himself.   *Genesis 28:16*

> I was in my own way.
> My thoughts, stories, habits and expectations
> Kept me distracted,
> Put me to sleep.

Mah nora ha makon hazeh.
How awesome is this place, how awesome is this moment.   *Genesis 28:17*

How will I remember this experience
And know that it was real?
How will I return again and again to awareness?
How will I continue to break through to what is true?

The Mystery called to Jacob:
Take notice, I am with you
And I will guard you wherever you go.   *Genesis 28:15*

Jacob set an intention:
If I seek God, if I seek the Mystery and can discern God's presence,
Then I will know the paths to follow,
Then I will have whatever I need to discern my way.

And Jacob gives us this gift:
At the edge of our minds,
In the realm beyond certainty,
Is our courageous imagination,
Our capacity to break through assumptions, doubts and fears
And behold possibilities.

At the edge of our minds,
In the realm beyond certainty,
Stands *sha'ar hashamayim,*   *Genesis 28:17*
A gateway to the Mystery,
An opening to be awake to the truths of our lives.

Sometimes we will duck.
Other times we will go to sleep.
And there will be moments
When we get out of our own way,
Break through the stories, expectations
And fears
That keep us distracted
And rise up awake and present.

Echoing Jacob we can say,
Mah nora ha makom hazeh.
How awesome is this place.
How awesome is this moment.

PRACTICE FOR THE WEEK

Sitting into the Moment

We bring ourselves to an awake posture – sitting in a way that allows our heart space to be open, resting our hands so as not to put strain on our necks or backs. Anchoring our attention on the breath as it moves through the body, we repeat the words Jacob called out in the experience of awareness: *Mah nora ha makom hazeh:* How awesome is this place.

As the breath rises and falls, we continue:
Mah nora ha makom hazeh.
Each time the attention wanders, (as it will),
we return to the present with the call:
Mah nora ha makom hazeh: How awesome is this place.

We close the sit by hearing the words the Infinite spoke to Jacob:
Take notice, I am with you and I will guard you wherever you go.

As we go about our day, we might want to repeat the phrase *Mah nora ha makom hazeh*, letting it be a *zecar*, a reminder, calling us to be present and awake to our encounters and experiences.

Vayishlach: Sending Forth

Alone by the river, Jacob wrestled through the night.
As dawn approached, he knew it was time to stop struggling.
But he could not let go.

He cried into the coming day —

I will not give up until I find a blessing in all this conflict and pain. Genesis 32:27

In that moment the one with whom he was wrestling asked,

What is your name?
He responded, Jacob.   Genesis 32:28

The last time Jacob had been asked this question he had answered:

I am Esau.   Genesis 27:19

This time Jacob told the truth
And from the truth flowed this blessing:

Your name shall not only be Jacob.   Genesis 32:29

> You will not only be the one who grasps,
> Who holds on,
> Who suffers because he wants things
> To be different from what they are.

Your name shall also be Yisrael –   Genesis 32:29
The one who wrestles with God.

> Also hear this name as *Yashar El,*
> The one who is *directed toward God,*
> The one who has the strength to set intentions,
> Follow them,
> And meet well whatever is encountered.

> The inclination to grasp and control,
> The strength to be fully with what is —
> Both of these capacities exist within you, Jacob was told.
> Notice when they occur,

Be aware of whom and what they serve,
And discover how to use them well.

Jacob walked into the new day limping,
His vulnerability revealed.

And he named this place of
Struggle,
Truth
And Blessing,
Peni-el — the Presence of God.   *Genesis 32:31*

PRACTICE FOR THE WEEK

Revealing and Being

Jacob told the truth and from the truth flowed blessing.
Jacob came out of hiding
And had an experience of such clarity and release
That when he finally encountered his brother Esau
He was able to say to him: *Looking at your face is like seeing the face of God.*
                                                  Genesis 33:10

We are *Beit Ya'acov*, the House of Jacob, and *B'nai Yisrael*, the Children of Israel. Within us are the tendencies to hide, to grasp, to cling, to struggle with who we are and who we wish we could be. Also within us is the capacity to go forward with intention and awareness and meet the encounters of our lives with honesty and wisdom.

Within us is the capacity to see in ourselves and each other the face of God.

This week we ask ourselves:
What truths am I struggling with?
What parts of my life am I keeping hidden?
What vulnerabilities am I afraid to reveal?

What is something I can share with someone that will help release some of the fear, shame, regret or pain that I am holding?

As we sit each day this week, we repeat God's first words to Jacob:
Hinei anochi imach
Take notice, I am with you, which can also be translated,
Take notice I am within you. Genesis 28:15

As we bring attention to the breath, we bring this phrase into our bodies: *Hinei anochi imach, Take notice, I am with you. Take notice I am within you,* gently repeating the phrase again and again.

Each time we notice that thoughts have arisen, with gentleness and strength, we bring ourselves back to the present and the call from the Infinite Presence: *Hinei anochi imach. I am with you, I am within you. Hinei anochi imach.*

We end our sit with these intentions:
I will walk into this day with all of who I am.
I will meet each encounter with compassion and generosity.

Vayeshev: Seeking to Settle

Jacob sought rest.
He yearned to settle,
To dwell in comfort and peace.

He sought relief from upheaval.
He wanted to stop questioning,
To cease wandering,
And be still.

But instead, Jacob's own vulnerabilities and human frailties
Brought contention and pain.

Jacob's favoring of his son Joseph
Created upheaval within the family
And resulted in jealousy and rage.

The family was torn apart,
Any hope of comfort and peace gone.

Even as we seek to settle,
Even as we yearn for calm and rest,
The mission of being human
Makes this difficult.
Feelings arise.
Thoughts emerge.
And our struggles, vulnerabilities and experiences
Get tangled.
We trip and fall,
Causing pain to ourselves and others.

Sometimes the fall is so severe
We land in a deep pit
And feel unable to rise.

Let us remember that
We all are vulnerable beings
Doing the best we can in each moment.

We all have dreams for our lives.
Visions and hopes of what might be.
And we all have experiences
That help us weave our dreams into reality.
And we all have experiences
That tear our dreams apart.

Let us be kind to ourselves and each other.
Let us treat each other with tenderness and care.

PRACTICE FOR THE WEEK

Sitting with Moment to Moment Awareness

We take our seats with the intention of sitting with calm, relaxed awareness.

Bringing ourselves to an awake, upright posture, we anchor the attention on the breath, watching as the breath is received and released. As we notice thoughts and feelings arise, we do our best to let them pass and return our attention to the breath and the present moment.

When we find ourselves following thoughts and stories, we return our attention to the breath with kindness, gentleness and care. Every distracting thought or story is an opportunity to practice kindness and strengthen our ability to return the attention to the present moment.

Miketz: From Endings

Joseph was forgotten.   *Genesis 40:23*

In the pit of prison,
In a land not his own,
Joseph was forgotten.

And then Joseph was remembered.

He was brought up from the dungeon,
Retrieved from the depths,
And recognized for who he was
And who he could become.

Pharaoh exclaimed,
Ruach elohim bo — The spirit of God is within him.
There is no one who can be found who is more wise or discerning than he.

Genesis 41:38-39

> This is a man who can see through dreams and images,
> Who can wade through misery and fear.
> This man is open to the Mystery
> And can see the Divine weaving the fabric of life.

And Pharaoh gave Joseph a new name — *Creator of Life.*
And gave him charge over the land of Egypt.

And Joseph grew
Powerful, abundant, fertile and strong.
Joseph grew,
And Joseph forgot.

He forgot his pain.
He forgot his hardships.
He forgot the bonds to his father's house.

Joseph forgot
Until his brothers appeared.
Seeking food and sustenance,
They asked for his help.

Bowing low to the ground,
They lay themselves down at the feet of the man
They did not know was their brother.

And then Joseph began to remember
And re-create
The narrative of his life:
    Beauty, loss,
    Love, betrayal,
    Jealousy, possibility,
    Scarcity, abundance,
    Dreams, uncertainty,
    Faith.

And, there within the brokenness,
Tucked between the cracks,
The Shining Mystery — the Presence of God.

And Joseph wept.
He wept as he struggled
With how to remember his life,
How to take all he had lost and all he had found
And weave together the many-colored threads
Into a story that would shine with meaning and purpose
And illuminate the mysterious pathways of God.

PRACTICE FOR THE WEEK

Ruach Elohim Bo — The Spirit of God is Within

This Torah portion reminds us that at times we need the help of others to recognize and live the fullness of our lives.

Joseph lost himself in the pain and challenges of his experiences. It was Pharaoh who saw Joseph's light, who recognized his potential. Pharaoh's perspective helped Joseph remember that the spirit of God is within him.

Pharaoh helped Joseph access the *chochmah* and *binah,* the wisdom and understanding that could flow through him into the world.

This week we sit into our fullness, aware of our beauty and brokenness. Taking our seats with awareness and bringing the attention to the breath, we say gently to ourselves,

Ruach Elohim Be — The spirit of God is within me. We repeat this phrase five to ten times, letting it move with the breath.

Then we call to our hearts and minds friends and members of our families and we say for each of them in turn:

Ruach Elohim Bo: The spirit of God is within him.
Ruach Elohim Bah: The spirit of God is within her.
Ruach Elohim Bam: The spirit of God is within them.

We call forth someone with whom there is need for healing and we say for them:

Ruach Elohim Bo: The spirit of God is within him.
Ruach Elohim Bah: The spirit of God is within her.
Ruach Elohim Bam: The spirit of God is within them.

We notice whoever arises in our minds and, for each person in turn, we say:

Ruach Elohim Bo: The spirit of God is within him.
Ruach Elohim Bah: The spirit of God is within her.
Ruach Elohim Bam: The spirit of God is within them.

As we prepare to close our sit, we set an intention that, throughout the day, we will seek to notice and call forth the goodness in ourselves and others.

Vayigash: Approaching

With trepidation and courage,
Judah drew close
To a complicated and frightening situation.
Urged on by love, commitment
And a deep sense of responsibility,
He made an offering of himself.

Drawing close
And speaking as much truth
As he was able,
Judah broke open hearts and minds.

His brother Joseph,
Who had,
Through the years,
Forgotten who he himself was,
Broke open
And rediscovered himself.

Through a well of tears,
Joseph revealed himself to his brothers
And assured them
That, within all misdeeds and brokenness,
Is the mysterious movement of God.

The brothers, so long filled with guilt and shame,
Stood silent in the face of truth.
Then, through the revelation of love and sorrow,
They broke open as well.

And Jacob, whose heart had been broken for so long,
Was reunited with his son Joseph,
And a connection that had been torn to shreds
Began to mend.

In the breaking open,
The past was not forgotten.

The hurt did not disappear.
But enough anger, guilt and fear
Was shattered
For forgiveness and love
To shine through.

PRACTICE FOR THE WEEK

Approaching

We take our seats and draw our attention to our posture and the sensations of being held by our cushions or chairs. After a few minutes of letting the attention rest on slow, calm deep breaths, we gently ask ourselves: How do I want to meet all that will arise in my heart, mind, body during the sit today? We might set an intention to approach each moment and each story or thought that arises in the mind with one of the following responses:

Curiosity
Calm
Courage
Kindness
Forgiveness
Love.

We do our best to choose one quality, and say to ourselves, *I approach this moment with* . . . .

We repeat this intention, again and again, letting it travel with the breath. Each time we notice that our minds have wandered to follow a thought or story, we say *I approach this thought, this story with* . . . .

We return our attention to the breath and say, *I approach this moment with* . . . .

As we close the sit, we encourage ourselves to approach each encounter of the day with the quality that arose for us during the sit.

Vayechi: Life

And Jacob lived.
And Jacob prepared to die.
With conscious intention,
He sought words of blessing, comfort and strength
To leave in his wake.

Jacob gathered his sons
So he could reveal to them
All that would happen
In days and years to come.
He wanted to assure them that,
Even though they would face great hardship and pain,
Generations to come would rise up
Into prosperity and peace.

But as Jacob began to speak, his mouth was stopped.
    For if he told his sons all that would happen,
    If he revealed to them all that would unfold,
    They would not be able to experience the fullness of their lives.

So, instead, Jacob uttered phrases
That created puzzles for each son
To solve for himself.
Jacob's silence and speech left his sons with the challenge
Of speaking their own lives into blessing.

At the end of his life,
Jacob spoke words that were clothed in mystery,
Reminding us that the path forward is revealed
Only as we go.

*

Joseph lived.
And Joseph prepared to die.
With conscious intention,
He sought words of blessing, comfort and strength
To leave in his wake.

He gathered his brothers
And said to them,
Do not be afraid.
Do not be afraid.
Our actions produce results
That are often different
From what we had intended.
Life unfolds as it will
And the Mystery is always present.
Joseph spoke these words with kindness right to their hearts.   *Genesis 50:19-21*

As the book of *Genesis* comes to a close,
We give thanks to our ancestors
Whose challenges, struggles and blessings
Have helped guide and shape our paths.
Their journeys invite us
To seek our own personal relationships
With the Infinite Mystery
And to discover the sacred
In the intricate patterns of our lives.

PRACTICE FOR THE WEEK
Gratitude

We take our seats, coming into an awake posture, letting our attention rest on the breath.

After a few minutes, we say to ourselves:
Modah/Modeh Ani — I am grateful.

We say this phrase with gentleness, taking notice of how this prayer feels in our bodies. Over and over, we repeat the prayer, *Modah/Modeh Ani — I am grateful,* letting the words travel on the breath.

Each time we notice our minds have wandered, we bring ourselves back to the present moment by returning to the breath and our prayer.

There are days when it is easy to say this prayer and there are times when turning toward gratitude causes pain and constriction. We do our best to notice this all with non-judgmental awareness and respond to whatever arises with gentleness and compassion.

As we close our sit, we set an intention to pause three times during the day to give thanks for something we notice or receive.

Shemot
The Book of Exodus

Shemot: Names

Moses was on his way,
Focused on where he was going,
Thinking he knew what his life would be,
When, all of a sudden,
He saw an amazing sight.
He turned and gazed long enough
To notice the bush that had been burning
Forever.

As he turned and paused,
Moses heard a voice from inside the earth,
From inside the fire,
From inside himself,
Call his name.

Moses' immediate response was:
Hineni, Here I am —   *Exodus 3:4*
        Present, willing, able.

Take off your shoes, the voice said,
For the place on which you stand is holy ground,   *Exodus 3:5*
        And I need you.

Realizing all he would need to let go of
And all he would need to become,
Moses cried,
        This is not what I asked for.
        I had other plans.
        I was on my way.
        This is not something I can or want to do.

The voice insisted:
        Your path is different
        From the one you had imagined.
        Feel your feet on this holy ground.

What is your name? Moses demanded,   *Exodus 3:13*
        You, who ask everything of me.

Ehyeh Asher Ehyeh, the voice answered,
I will be that I will be.   *Exodus 3:14*

    Wherever you are, there I am.
    I am expansive potential,
    Infinite possibility.
    I am all that is and all that can be
    And I am calling you forward.

Our paths unfold from here.
The earth we stand upon is holy ground,
And the bush is burning.

It is our inheritance
To look, to pause,
To listen,
To veer from certainty,
From habit,
From expectations,
And see the bush aflame.

It is our inheritance
To let the fire
Fuel our imagination,
Inspire our spirit,
And arouse our commitment,
To step forward
Into the truth of our lives
And offer ourselves
For healing,
For blessing,
For goodness,
For peace.

PRACTICE FOR THE WEEK

Hineni: Here I am

When Moses turned and gazed at the bush, he heard his name called *b'toch ha'aish,* from within the flames. His immediate response was *Hineni — here I am —* present to whatever this moment asks. With this response, Moses declared he would find the strength and willingness to rise into whatever was asked of him.

This week, we sit each day with the intention of calling ourselves present so we can be of service to ourselves and others.

We begin our sit by letting our attention rest on the breath, feeling it move throughout our bodies. After a few moments, we hear the call *Hineni — here I am —* rise within us. We repeat *Hineni* again and again, letting it travel on the breath, feeling its sensation throughout our bodies. Each time we notice that our minds have wandered, we give thanks for noticing and come back to the breath and the call, *Hineni.*

At the close of the sit, we set an intention to pause a few times during the day and call ourselves present by saying: *Hineni, Here I am.*

Vaera: I Appeared

In a time of great hardship, amid oppression and pain,
The Infinite appeared to Moses
And made a promise to him and his people:

I will take you out of bondage.
I will free you from serving what is not true.
I will call you present.
And I will bring you into relationship with all life.   *Exodus 6:6*

I will reveal myself beyond anything that has ever been seen,
Understood,
Or experienced.

I will reveal myself in my entirety,
Without limitation,
Without end.

And you will have no doubt
That I am here.

But the people,
Hearts broken by cruelty,
Souls beaten down by tyranny and fear,
Were unable to listen,
To imagine,
To receive.

All they could do was cry out
And turn away in pain.

But the One would not be deterred:

Reach for me wherever you are, said the One.
When you turn toward your fears, you will see me.
You will find me in pain, in sadness and despair.
Under the burdens of shame and anger, look for me.
I am present.
I am here.

And you will find me as you open yourselves to each other,
As you widen your circles and offer your hands.

The road is long,
Winding and often narrow,
The signs sometimes treacherous and fierce,

But I am here
And will be forever.

Seek me,
See me,
And Live.

PRACTICE FOR THE WEEK
The One Breath of All Life

We begin by bringing our attention to our bodies, noticing
our posture and where we place our hands. We take notice of
where our bodies meet our chairs or cushions and we notice the
sensations of our feet or legs on the floor.

After a few moments, we bring our attention to the breath,
watching, feeling the sensation of breath as it fills our bodies.
We feel the breath in our torsos, our arms and hands. We feel the
breath in our stomachs and feel it as it reaches down into our legs
and feet. We feel the breath in our shoulders, our necks, our faces
and the crowns of our heads.

Watching, noticing the breath move throughout the body, we set
an intention to know the breath as the One Breath of All Life, the
One Breath that fills all beings and enlivens all creation. We set
an intention to feel the One Breath move through us, calling us
present.

When we notice that our attention has wandered, we call ourselves
back by returning to the breath, feeling the sensation of the One
Breath fill and enliven our bodies.

Bo: Come Toward

The plagues have been raging
And the Infinite calls,
Come.
Step Toward.
Ready yourself to leave all that has been,
Mark your *mezzuzot,* your doorposts, with blood.
And make a commitment
To remember,
Always,
This journey of becoming.

The Pharaoh waits,
Moses approaches,
And God calls:

Come toward me.   *Exodus 10:1*

Come toward the hardened heart,
Come toward your terror, your pain,
Toward the nightmare,
The cry,
And you will find me here.

And the heart will crack open
And you will emerge
Free.

The soul stumbles and cries:
Is it possible to break through without shattering?
Without wreaking havoc?
Without spilling blood?

The Infinite responds:

Look at tender new plants,
Tiny green shoots,
Who, challenging all reason,
Defying the pull of gravity,

42

Push through the hard-packed earth.
Break through thick slabs of concrete,
And emerge
Fresh and new.

I am wherever you seek me:
In hardened hearts,
In tender shoots,
In blood-soaked freedom,
In the possibilities of a new life.

Let there be a sign upon your hands
And a remembrance between your eyes. Exodus 13:9

So always will you remember
There is a way through narrowness,
Constriction,
And pain,
And it is I —The Infinite Mystery — calling you forward.

I am within the pain
And I am on the other side.
The journey is always
And I am calling you home.

PRACTICE FOR THE WEEK

Held by the Divine Presence

We begin the sit by bringing our attention to the body and breath.
Following the breath, we steady ourselves into an awake and
upright posture. Noticing where and how we place our hands, we
make sure our shoulders are back so the heart space is open.

After a few minutes we say to ourselves:
I am held by the Divine Presence. I am sheltered in a loving embrace.

Even as the mind races, even as tensions rise, we say:
I am held by the Divine Presence. I am sheltered in a loving embrace.

To whatever thought, feeling, story arises in the mind, we respond: *I am held by the Divine Presence. I am sheltered in a loving embrace.*

With gentle strength, we repeat this phrase again and again.

We close our sit by saying:
May all beings be held by the Divine Presence, sheltered in a loving embrace.

Beshallach: In Sending Forth

How do we leave the narrow places?
The hardened hearts?
The constricted minds?

How do we go forth from habits,
From behaviors,
From beliefs,
That are so old, so ingrained,
We think this is who we are?

The Israelites were led the long way around —
By way of the wilderness,
By way of the sea,
Because it is so difficult to leave what has been,
Even when what has been is painful,
Even when what has been
Is no longer of service,
Is no longer true.

Our ancestors stood at the shores of the sea,
Frightened and desperate.
They wanted to run, to hide, to turn back,
But they stepped forward
And the waters opened.

And together they walked across the sea on dry ground.
And there, on the other side,
They experienced the power that had delivered them.

And they had faith in Moses
And in the Mystery they called God.   *Exodus 14:31*

By the shores of the sea, on the edge of the unknown,
They lifted their voices, sang and rejoiced:

My strength and God's song is the way into the expanse.   *Exodus 15:2*
The Mystery is forever.   *Exodus 15:18*
Let us sing and dance with the One.   *Exodus 15:20-21*

And then, only moments later,
Fear crept back.
Doubt, despair, and desperation took hold.

> Where are we?
> What have we done?
> We can't live from here.
> The only thing to do,
> Our only safe choice,
> Is to return to what has been,
> To go back to what is known.

The Mystery responded by teaching the people about Shabbat:

Six days you will work, gather and seek.
And on the seventh day you will stop, rest
And simply be.   *Exodus 16:23*

> This practice will teach you balance and reverence
> And help you find your faith, courage and strength.
> As you make stopping a ritual, your vision will clear
> And you will be more able to see where you have been,
> And where it is you are meant to go.

How do we leave the narrow places?
The hardened hearts?
The constricted minds?
How do we go forth from what is no longer true?

Like our ancestors, we come to the edge of the sea
Again and again.

There are no easy answers,
No guaranteed paths,
And no end to the journey.

But the gift of Shabbat is offered.
Pause, the Mystery calls.
Make a commitment to stop, to reflect, to calm the mind
And be wherever you are.
This practice will help you return to a spacious perspective,

Discover your wise and generous hearts,
And discern the path to walk.

Stop. Rest. Pause. Be.
You will find your strength.
Stop. Rest. Pause. Be.
And you will hear your song.

PRACTICE FOR THE WEEK

I am the One, your Healer

Exodus 15:26

After the Israelites crossed the sea, they tasted the bitterness of all they had been through and their fear and despair returned. In that moment, God, the Infinite Mystery, urged them to trust that the bitter becomes sweet with commitment and devotion to practice. Practice helps us see more clearly and return to a perspective that encourages faith and possibility.

The Mystery calls: Listen to the voice of the One, set intentions, do your practice, for I am the Infinite, your Healer.   *Exodus 15: 24-26*

As we practice this week, we sit with this call from the Mystery: *I am the One, your Healer.*

Beginning each sit in an awake posture, we focus the attention on the breath. After a few minutes we hear this call: *I am the One, your Healer.* We repeat this phrase, letting it travel with the breath. When our attention wanders, we call ourselves back to presence by returning to this phrase: *I am the One, your Healer.*

At the close of the sit, we give thanks and set an intention for how we want to go forth into the day.

Yitro: Jethro

Our ancestors crossed the sea and journeyed to the wilderness of Sinai.
Three days of preparation
And they stood at a quaking mountain.

A *shofar* wailed.
Thunder streaked across the sky.
Lightening roared.
Smoke rose, enveloping the mountain.
Fire descended
And all the earth shook.

Then the world disappeared.
All distinction vanished.
There was no I, no you, no tree, bird, water or rock.
There was only One
One breath,
One life,
Only One,
Infinite,
Eternal.

Then the *shofar* wailed again
And the world in all its uniqueness rushed back:
Bird, wind, desert, sky.
And all of us stood
With the One breath still on our lips.

And we knew.
We knew
The One inside the many,
The One beyond anything that could be seen or known,
And we trembled in awe.

We stepped back from the mountain.
We turned from the fire
And we listened.
We listened to the One reverberate in our hearts.
And in the silence, we heard the Mystery call:

1. I am, I was, I will be. I am the unfolding of all that is.
   I am constant transformation calling you forward to be.

2. Do not give yourself to falsehood.
   Do not seek to arrest me in motion or create me with your own
   hands. Be with uncertainty. Allow mystery.

3. Do not use a Divine name to make false promises.
   Do not use sacred teachings to lift up a destructive path.

4. Rest, Stop, Pause. Be. Honor creation. Declare your freedom.
   Rest and allow others to rest as well.

5. Honor your parents. Honor your ancestors.
   Honor those upon whose shoulders you stand.

6. Do not murder.

7. Do not betray.

8. Do not steal.

9. Do not use the power of words to hurt or destroy.

10. Feel the fullness of your life. Do not be led astray by comparing
    yourself to others. Do not get lost in desiring what others have.
    Be content, be fulfilled with what your life brings.   *Exodus 20:1-14*

The soul trembles awake.
The mountain continues to flame.
And always the Infinite calls:

Practice.
Make an altar of the earth.
Raise up peace and well-being for all,
And know that every moment of remembering the One
In the midst of the many
Is a moment of blessing.   *Exodus 20:21*

PRACTICE FOR THE WEEK
Receiving

The first word of the Ten Utterances is: *Anochi,* I am.
I am present. I am here. I am always.
I am in every thing, in every moment.

This week we sit into this Eternal call.

Beginning by resting our attention on the breath, we call ourselves present.

Following the breath, we bring awareness to our bodies, noticing how we are held by our chairs or cushions, feeling our feet or legs meet the floor, noticing the position of our hands. We bring our shoulders back so the heart space is open. We relax our jaws, our mouths and faces.

After a few minutes, we listen for the call *Anochi* deep within our bodies. We feel this call rise and fall with the breath. We watch as *Anochi* fills us and pours through us into the world. We hear the call *Anochi* again and again and again. Every time the attention wanders, we bring ourselves back by hearing and feeling the One speak to our hearts, our minds, our souls, our bodies: *Anochi,* I am — Present, Here, Always — *Anochi.*

Mishpatim: Practices

Across the sea,
Down from the mountain,
Now in the *midbar* — the vast, uncharted wilderness —
How do we discern the path?

For so long, we served the Pharaoh.
We bowed to all that oppressed us,
To all that kept our hearts hardened and our souls enslaved.
For so long, we were in a narrow place
Where the confines of demands, and "shoulds" and "have tos"
Shaped our thoughts, our actions, our deeds.

The soul enslaved can't help but be narrow,
Can't help but be driven by its own stories, its own pain.
The soul enslaved puts itself at the center
And can't find the capacity to care about anything or anyone else.

The Mystery calls:
Free yourself by serving me.
Discern the path
By serving what is ultimate,
By giving yourself to what is true.

The soul cries:
How will we recognize the way?
How will we break through what has been for so long?
How will we find and keep returning to what is ultimate?

Make a commitment to practice, the Mystery instructs:

Set intentions,
Be disciplined.
Devote your time and energy to this effort.

Take on practices that call for focus and awareness,
Practices that challenge habitual behavior,
And help cultivate an expansive perspective and calm mind.

Take on practices that direct your attention beyond yourself,
That call you into relationship
And awaken concern and responsibility for the well-being of others.

Make a commitment to practice
And you will know I am with you, the Mystery calls.

At times the paths will be narrow
And the way forward confusing and unclear.
Do your best to stay true to your commitments
And when you fall short,
Practice forgiveness and compassion.

And look for me in the *midbar*, in the vast uncharted wilderness.
Know that I am there.
Practice so as to notice me.
For behold, I send messengers before you to guard you on your way and bring
you to the place I have prepared.   *Exodus 23:20*

PRACTICE FOR THE WEEK

Noticing

We begin our sit mindful of our bodies. We notice our posture. We feel where our bodies meet our chairs or cushions, the placement of our hands, our legs, our feet. Following the breath, we notice the sensations in our faces, our necks and shoulders. We follow the breath into the torso and down each arm into the fingertips. We breathe into the belly and watch as the breath travels down the legs and into the feet. As we become aware of any pain or tension in the body, we breathe into these areas with kindness.

We set an intention to not follow the thoughts and stories that arise. Each time we notice that the attention has fixed on a thought, we return our attention to the breath — noticing, feeling, experiencing the sensations of the breath as it moves through our bodies.

At the end of the sit, we offer thanks. As we go about our day, we notice:

Through my decisions and actions, what am I serving?

Where am I finding messengers, guidance?

How am I being a messenger or a guide?

Terumah: Gifts

We stood at the mountain
And experienced the One in smoke and in fire.
We heard the One call to us
In thunder and in the quaking of earth.
Awestruck, we responded by creating rules and laws to live by,
Statutes that would return us again and again to the One.

And now the Mystery calls:
*Make for me a sacred place that I might dwell **within** you.*   *Exodus 25:8*

Bring me gifts of what you love,
Gifts of beauty, radiance and joy.
Bring me gifts of what you value, what you hold most precious and dear.
And make for me a sacred place that I might dwell within you.

Know that it is not your gold and silver I desire,
Nor your dolphin skins, copper or jewels.
What I am asking for is your generosity,
Your willingness to give.

For I am seeking intimacy:
Make for me a sacred place by opening your heart
And lifting up the work of your hands.
Create a space for my presence
By honoring your beauty and offering your gifts.

I come to you on eagles' wings and in the silence of each breath.
Cultivate your wise and generous heart
So you will seek me and find me in the unfolding of your life.

*Make for me a sacred place that I might dwell **among** you.*   *Exodus 25:8*

Fashion for me a community filled with intention and care,
A community that appreciates beauty
And inspires gifts of the heart.

Make for me a community that lifts up its values,
Honors its traditions,

And is willing to change and grow,
A community that recognizes the holy in the faces of each other.

When we were on the mountain, I showed you the way.
I revealed to you the patterns through which you bring me to dwell.
And while I am present in the boundless, the spectacular,
The transcendent, the grand,
My desire is to live among you
In the intricacies of your everyday.

So please,
Light your lamps,
Set your tables,
And invite me in.

PRACTICE FOR THE WEEK

Creating Sacred Space

We begin our sit with careful attention to our posture. Following the breath as it flows into the body, we gently pull our shoulders back so the heart space is open. We relax our jaws and the muscles in our faces. We breathe down our arms and into the placement of the hands. We watch as the breath moves down our legs and into our feet.

After a few minutes, we ask ourselves to hear the call:
I dwell within you.

Repeating this call again and again we imagine ourselves as dwellings for the Divine. With each breath, the Divine fills us, fashioning a space for itself.

Following the breath, we notice where in the body the Divine lands, where in the body the space opens for the Divine dwelling, and we breathe into these spaces. We also take notice of the places in the body that feel tight or constricted and breathe into these places with gentleness and care. With each breath, the Divine is present and with each breath, the sacred dwelling is fashioned and strengthened.

When we notice our attention has wandered, we call ourselves back by returning to the breath and the call: *I dwell within you.*

At the end of the sit, we set an intention that, as we go about our day, we will remember that the Divine dwells within us and within every person we encounter.

Tetzaveh: Connect

The Mystery continues to seek us.

Open to me, the One calls.
Wrap me as a sacred garment around you.
Feel me in the threads of connection and possibility.
Hear me as a soft bell calling you awake.
Rest me upon your hand and your heart so I can help guide your actions.
Place me upon your foot so you will know which way to turn.
Place me before your eyes, so you will see me in all.

I continually seek your presence, the One calls.
And because I desire you, because I yearn to surround you,
I give you *mitzvot* — instructions that will help us find each other:

Raise up your light, always.
From evening to morning, in times of challenge and blessing,
Raise up your light.
This is a constant practice.
Let yourself shine.

Cultivate a wise heart.
I have filled you with the spirit of wisdom.
Weave this spirit into your life.
Treasure your relationships,
Honor your family, your community.
Place their well-being upon your heart,
And become the wisdom that flows from here.

Practice awareness.
Remember that in every moment you stand before the One,
In relationship with all who have come before you and all who will
come after.

Nurture discernment.
Be deliberate and thoughtful as you make choices.
Turn to the spirit for help and guidance.
Listen to the wise counsel of the heart.

Offer your well-being to each other:
Lift up your spirit,
Share your gifts.
Let your blessings be for the benefit of all.
And I will meet you at each opening,
And I will speak with you,
And I will clothe you in my glory.
For I seek your presence always.   *Exodus 29:42-3*

PRACTICE FOR THE WEEK
Directing the Heart

In this week's portion, we read how Aaron prepared for his role as spiritual leader by placing upon his heart a breastplate inscribed with the names of the twelve Israelite tribes. Inside the breastplate were Urim and Thummim, ritual objects that called him present and connected him to spirit, wisdom and clarity.

For our practice this week, we ask ourselves what words, phrases or images we can place upon our hearts to help call us present and guide us in seeing clearly and making wise, compassionate choices.

As we sit each day, we begin by letting our attention rest on the breath, following it as it moves through the body. We notice the sensations of the breath in the chest, shoulders, neck, face, arms, torso and legs.

After a few minutes we ask ourselves, with kindness and patience: What word, image or phrase do I place upon my heart today?

We repeat this question gently to ourselves again and again, noticing what arises.

When a word, phrase or image does appear, we do our best to welcome it as a sacred gift, to notice it with interest and curiosity and not follow any stories about it the mind might create.

We place the word, phrase or image upon the heart and repeat it over and over. Each time we notice that our attention has wandered, we return to the word, phrase or image. We place it upon the heart and feel its vibration and sensation.

When a word, phrase or image does not arise, we do our best to notice this with interest and curiosity and we keep returning our attention to the breath. We notice the vibrations and sensations of the breath as it moves through the chest and surrounds the heart.

At the close of the sit, we offer thanks.

If a word, phrase or image did appear, we set an intention to place it upon our hearts and return to it again and again as we go about our day.

At the end of the week, we might want to spend some time reflecting on the words, phrases and images that arose and wonder about wearing them as sacred garments.

Ki Tisa: What We Lift Up

We were in the desert,
Waiting for Moses to return.
He had gone to the mountain
And promised to be back.

Waiting in the vastness of the wilderness,
We grew so afraid.

Doubt crept in.
Terror seized our minds
And we grasped for certainty.

We reached for something we could hold onto,
Something tangible and sure.

We took the gold from our ears,
We collected our jewelry, our treasures,
And we fashioned for ourselves a golden calf,
And we called this creature of our own making:
Holy One, our God.

And we danced and sang:
This is the God who brought us out of Egypt.
This is the One who sustains us.
This One,
Whom we have made,
And who will never change,
This is the Holy One, our God.

And for a moment,
We were so sure.

But everything changes.
Certainty is fleeting
And worshiping the work of our hands leads us astray.

When Moses returned from the mountain,
With the tablets engraved with the mystery of the Infinite's presence,
He could not come into the camp.

For the tablets inscribed with the Infinite could not enter a place
Where fear ruled,
And permanence was worshipped.
So these tablets, our gift of the Eternal Mystery,
Were shattered.

We still carry the brokenness with us,
The sharp and torn fragments causing pain.

Yet between the shattered pieces
The Mystery shines,
With compassion, grace,
Patience and love.

There is a place for you with me, the Mystery assures us.   *Exodus 33:21*

I am standing right here beside you.
Listen. Hear me call my name:

All Being, All Being, the Expanse of Compassion and Graciousness,
Patience, the Abundance of Love and Truth,
Extending Generosity through time and space,
Lifting up Guilt and Despair from the Depths of Misdeeds,
And making you free.   *Exodus 34:5-7*

Don't be deterred by brokenness, the One calls.
Don't be stopped by regrets, by mistakes or misdeeds.
Call on the love that is eternal,
The compassion that extends beyond time and space.

Feel the light of the Infinite
And rise and live.
I am standing with you, the Mystery calls
And always there is a place for you with Me.

PRACTICE FOR THE WEEK
Calling on the Name of the Infinite

In this week's portion, the Infinite proclaims: I am standing with you and this is my name: *Love, Compassion, Forgiveness.*

For our practice this week, we call on this name.

We begin our sit by bringing ourselves to an awake posture, taking notice of where we place our feet and our hands, drawing our shoulders back so the heart space is open. Following the breath, we relax our jaws, our necks, our shoulders. We watch as the breath moves down our arms into our hands, down our torsos, into our legs and feet.

After a few minutes, we return our attention to the heart space and begin to repeat the name of the Infinite:
Love, Compassion, Forgiveness.

We let this name travel on our breath and feel its vibration in our bodies. Over and over again, we call on the name:
Love, Compassion, Forgiveness. Each time we notice that our minds have wandered into thoughts, stories, doubts, fears, we bring ourselves back by gently returning to our breath and calling on the name the One has proclaimed:
Love, Compassion, Forgiveness.

At the close of the sit, we give thanks and set an intention that, as we go about our day, we will see ourselves and others with eyes of love, compassion and forgiveness.

Vayakhel: Gathering

Everything moves so fast.
Even when we are paying attention,
Days become weeks,
Weeks become years.
A lifetime goes by in a moment.

This is one of the many reasons to pause, to stop,
To rest.

Six days a week, engage in work.
Involve yourself with the doings of the world.
And on the seventh day,
Pause, stop, rest.
This, the Torah says, is a matter of life and death.

The practice of pausing, stopping, resting
Keeps our souls alive.
It encourages wonder
And renews our energy and strength.

Pausing, stopping, resting
Keeps us mindful and aware
Of the constant flow of time
And helps us be discerning
Of what we do with this precious gift.

Pausing, stopping, resting
Honors creation
And helps us remember
That we are a part of the unfolding of creation
Along with all of life.

So gather together, the Torah calls,
And support each other in pausing.
Gather together and build sanctuaries in time.

Adorn time with love,
With purpose,
With commitment and joys.

Fashion time with community,
With wisdom,
With heart-centered awareness.
And pause on the seventh day
To refresh and renew your soul.

Together,
Make sacred the gifts of time
Through stopping, resting, being.

This, the Torah says, is essential,
A matter of life and death.

PRACTICE FOR THE WEEK

Pausing

We take our seats with the intention of pausing from the busyness and demands of life.

With the attention resting on the breath, we settle into each moment and say gently to ourselves, *I am right here, right now.*

We remind ourselves that there is nothing else we need to do. We are free to be present in moment-to-moment awareness, *right here, right now.* Every time we notice that thoughts and stories are arising and demanding our attention, we say gently to these thoughts, *not now* and return our attention to the breath and the awareness that we are *right here, right now.*

At the close of the sit, we give thanks for the gift of being able to pause and set an intention to take opportunities to move slowly as we go about our day.

Pekudei: Accounting

As the book of Exodus draws to a close, the work to build
The *Mishkan*,
The dwelling for the Sacred Presence, is complete.

The *Mishkan* was created with generosity and love.
It was fashioned by wise hearts and skillful hands.
Every gift was honored
And each unique offering was of use.

The *Mishkan* was placed at the center of the community
And the *Kavod Hashem*, the Glory of the Presence,
Emanated from within.
The Presence filled the camp and spoke to each heart:

I dwell within and among you.
Fashion your lives so as to know me,
Weave your days so as to return to me again and again and again.

Look for me everywhere.
I am in your words and your deeds.
I come through your intentions and the work of your hands.

Find me at all times.
I am with you in clarity and well-being.
And I am with you in confusion, loneliness and fear.

Watch for me in the darkness.
See me in the light.
I am the guide on the journey.
And I am the journey itself.

Lift up the *Mishkan*.
Carry the sacred center wherever you go.
And practice so as to remember
That, in all your travels,
Wherever you go,
Wherever you are,
I am there.

PRACTICE FOR THE WEEK

Opening to Guidance

We begin our sit noticing the sensations in the body as we find our seats.

We notice how it feels to take this time to pause and settle into our posture. Following the breath, we notice the sensations in the chest and the shoulders. We let our attention travel down the arms and into the hands. We feel the breath in the neck, head and face. And we follow the breath back down the torso into the legs and feet.

After a few minutes, with gentleness and love, we say to ourselves:
I am guided on my journey.

Again and again, we say:
I am guided on my journey.

When thoughts, stories, doubts arise,
we gently return to the breath and our prayer:
I am guided on my journey.

After a short while, we notice the breath is the guidance. The breath is the spirit coming through us, filling us, guiding us to the presence of each moment. We follow the breath, repeating the prayer.
I am guided on my journey.

At the end of the sit, we give thanks and set an intention for how we would like to travel through the day. We say to ourselves:

May I go forward into this day with _____ .

Vayikra
The Book of Leviticus

Vayikra: Callings

As we enter the third book of the Torah,
The Mystery calls:
Here in the wilderness,
On your journeys of becoming,
Draw close to me.
Feel your strength,
Call forth your humility,
And set an intention to align yourself with the Highest Will.

Remember that your life is a gift
And everything you are
And everything you have been given
Is yours to share.

Make your life an offering,
And draw close to me.

Give thanks.
Offer gratitude for the bounty and blessings.
Look for opportunities to be grateful.
Acknowledge moments of well-being.

Engage in forgiveness.
Acknowledge the hurt and pain you have caused
And let this awareness guide you
In seeking healing and repair.

Practice compassion and understanding.
Let it release you from anger, resentment and regret.

Honor your gifts.
Enjoy your uniqueness.
Make an offering of your talents, your distinctions,
Your vulnerabilities and delights.

Let yourself be known.

The way through the wilderness can be confusing.
It is easy to get lost.
Draw close,
The Mystery calls,
By setting intentions and lifting up prayers.

Let your practices,
Deeds,
Doubts,
Mistakes and
Blessings
Be your offerings.

In every moment, the Mystery proclaims, I am here.
Draw close.

PRACTICE FOR THE WEEK
Offerings

We take our seats with awareness and let the attention rest on the breath. Following the breath as it moves in the body, we watch as it travels through the head, face and neck. We feel the breath in the shoulders and watch as it moves down the arms into each finger. We follow the breath as it fills the torso and stomach and as it travels down the legs into each toe. With the attention on the breath, we feel the power and beauty of the life that we are. Breathing into the whole body, we set an intention to offer ourselves for blessing.

After a few minutes of focusing on the breath, we call out this song of the psalmist:

I am my prayer to you,
Aligned with the Highest Will in this very moment.
With great love and generosity,
Receive me with the truth of your presence.   Psalm 69:14

Over and over, we declare that our lives are our offerings
by repeating the first part of the verse:
I am my prayer to you, I am my prayer to you.

When we notice the mind has wandered, when we become aware
that stories, thoughts, doubts, resistance have arisen, we return to
the song of the psalmist:
I am my prayer to you.

We breathe into our shoulders, our torsos, our legs:
I am my prayer to you.
We breathe into our hearts, our arms, our hands:
I am my prayer to you.
To any thoughts, stories or confusion:
I am my prayer to you.
To impatience, doubt, shame and fear:
I am my prayer to you.
Whatever arises, whatever appears, we respond:
I am my prayer to you.

At the end of the sit, we repeat the whole verse again and set an
intention for how we would like to take this prayer into our day:

I am my prayer to you,
aligned with the Highest Will in this very moment.
With great love and generosity,
receive me with the truth of your presence.

Tzav: Commands

A fire shall continuously burn on the altar.   *Leviticus 6:6*

We have been called into holy service:
Keep the fires burning.

Every evening,
Lay on the altar the offerings of the day
And keep the fires burning.
Every morning,
Renew the commitment
To tend the flames
And keep the fires burning.

Tend the fire that appeared in the burning bush.
We were in the wilderness,
On our way,
When, out of a bush filled with flames,
The Holy One called and said,
I need you.   *Exodus 3:2-4*

> I need you as my partner.
> I need you to turn toward your passion and your courage
> So I can come into the world through your words,
> Your deeds,
> And the work of your hands.
>
> I need you.
> And I have great faith in you.
> I see who you are,
> I know your capacities.
>
> Take this fire
> And tend these flames.
> I need you.

A fire shall continuously burn on the altar.   *Leviticus 6:6*

Tend the fire encountered on Mount Sinai,
When the Holy One spoke to us
From the midst of flames,
*Intimately, directly—face **within** face,*   *Deuteronomy 5:4*
And gave us our Torah,
Revealed to us our strengths, our potentials, our gifts, our possibilities.

>   Take this fire,
>   Tend these flames.

A fire shall continuously burn on the altar   *Leviticus 6:6*
>   Keep the fires burning
>   By living with truth and passion,
>   By speaking with courage and acting with integrity.

Keep the fires burning
With practice,
With devotion,
Through commitment and care.

Every evening,
Give thanks for the gifts of the day.
Every morning, hear the Holy One call:
I have great faith in you.
And keep the fires burning.

We are called into holy service.
Let us tend the flames
And keep the fires burning.

PRACTICE FOR THE WEEK

Tending the Eternal Fire

> We bring ourselves to an awake posture and draw our attention
> to the breath, following the breath as it comes into the body
> and as it is released.
>
> After a few minutes of centering in this way,
> we place upon our hearts the call from the morning prayers:
>
> *Raba Emunatecha*, the Holy One saying to us:
> *I have great faith in you.*
>
> Over and over again, we hear this call:
> *Raba Emunatecha, I have great faith in you.*
>
> We let this prayer travel on the breath and fill the body:
> *Raba Emunatecha, I have great faith in you.*
>
> With each breath, the prayer moves into the chest,
> the torso, the legs and feet:
> *Raba Emunatecha, I have great faith in you.*
>
> The prayer fills the shoulders, neck, face and head
> and travels down the arms, into the hands:
> *Raba Emunatecha, I have great faith in you.*
>
> When we notice that stories have arisen, when we experience
> resistance, doubts, or fears, we let the Holy One call us back
> to the moment with gentleness and love:
> *Raba Emunatecha, I have great faith in you.*
>
> *At the end of the sit, we offer gratitude and*
> *set an intention for the day:*
> *May I trust that the Holy One has great faith in me.*
> *Today, may I tend the fires of _____.*

Shemini: The Eighth Day

Moses spoke to the people:
Today the Infinite One will appear to you.   *Leviticus 9:4*

Our ancestors brought offerings of calves and goats,
Lambs and oxen,
Rams, incense and oil.
They drew close and stood together before the One.

Aaron and his sons took these offerings
And laid them upon the altar.

The fires rose,
The flames swirled,
The altar was engulfed by heat and smoke.

All day, the offerings smoldered.
Fat sizzled,
Blood was dashed upon the altar.
The flames kept rising
And everything that was brought to the altar was consumed.

After some time, Aaron lifted his hands toward the people
And blessed them
And the Presence of the One appeared to all.
A consuming fire came forth
And the people fell on their faces in awe.

Out of this moment,
Aaron's sons, *Nadav* and *Avihu*, stepped forward.
They placed incense on their fire pans
And offered *aish zera*, a strange fire.

Then a consuming fire came forth
And *Nadav* and *Avihu* died
In the Presence of the One.

We do not know the meaning
Of strange fire

Or if *Nadav* and *Avihu* were being punished
Or blessed by the consuming flames.

And we ask:
What do we do when faced with mystery,
When faced with what we can never understand?
What do we do when faced with catastrophe,
When even the best intentions and heartfelt actions
Bring forth results that leave us trembling and afraid?

There is no easy answer,
No sure way through.

There is, though, the power of presence.
Let us remember to draw close to each other
And make an offering of our presence.

With words,
With a touch,
With silence, with a glance,
Let our presence appear.
Let our presence go forth.
Let our presence to each other be sturdy and strong.

Let our presence be an offering in the face of the Mystery
And a balm for the consuming fires of pain, devastation, hardship
and fear.

PRACTICE FOR THE WEEK

Calling Ourselves Present

We take our seats and set an intention to be present to the moment.

Resting the attention on the breath, we notice the sensations of being held by our chairs or cushions. We take notice of where we place our hands and how our legs and feet are positioned. And we call ourselves present: present to breath, present to the moment.

Each time we notice that our attention has wandered and our minds are off somewhere else, we give thanks for noticing and call ourselves back, back to the breath, back to the moment. We can even view the arising of thoughts and stories in our minds as gifts, opportunities to remember to call ourselves back to the present moment.

At the close of the sit, we give thanks for calling ourselves present and set an intention that, as we go about our day, we will stop three times, be conscious of our breath and call ourselves present to the moment.

Tazria: Seeds

The natural inclination of the human being is to seek harmony,
To find balance, to revel in beauty.
And of course, there are so many things in life
That knock us around, mix us up, and leave us unsettled.

Sometimes we are thrown off balance by joyful surprises,
Spectacular sensations,
Wondrous events.
Other times our equilibrium is upset from fear, pain,
Challenging encounters and difficult situations.
And sometimes it is just the natural flow of what a day requires
That knocks us off center.

Finding Balance,
Seeking Harmony,
Is a practice we do again and again.

Listen to the body, the tradition teaches,
Take notice of what it is telling you.

What is the body communicating through
its sensations, its manifestations and needs?
What can be discerned from how tired, awake,
stressed, strained, or relaxed the body feels?

Tradition teaches that when we listen to the body,
We realize there are times for us to be outwardly engaged
And times for us to focus inward.

When we are awake to what the body is communicating,
We discover that there are times for us
To be in connection
And there are times
When it is important for us to separate ourselves.

This discernment can be challenging.
The signs from the body are not always clear
And interpreting what the body is communicating

Is difficult when we feel vulnerable,
When emotions erupt and the mind is confused or inflamed.

Yet the tradition is insistent:
Sometimes it is best to be in relationship
And other times it is imperative we step away.
The body can help us discern what it is true for us to do.

Finding Balance,
Seeking Harmony,
Is a practice that requires motion.
We step, shift, realign,
Finding the center again and again.

The body has secrets to tell,
Wisdom to share.
May its guidance come with gentleness and clarity,
Well-being and good health.

PRACTICE FOR THE WEEK
Mindful Attention to the Body

We begin our sit mindful of our posture, intentional of how we place our feet and where we place our hands. After a few centering breaths, we set an intention to be mindful of the sensations in our bodies.

With gentleness and curiosity, we notice anywhere in the body that feels strained, tense or painful. When we find a place of tightness or pain, we breathe into it with kindness, feeling the sensations, noticing the contours, shape, textures and colors of the tension or pain.

If stories, thoughts, or fears arise in relationship to the pain, we do our best not to follow them. We acknowledge that a story is arising and, returning to the breath, send kindness and love into the tense or painful places.

After a while, we follow the breath as it moves throughout the whole body, noticing how each part of the body feels as we attend to it.

We notice what it feels like to have the breath fill our lungs, our chests, our torsos. We feel the breath reaching into the shoulders, the neck, the face and head. We feel the breath move down the back, into the pelvis and down the legs into the feet.

When we are ready, each of us asks our body if there is anything it would like to tell us.

We ask this question with tenderness and love, knowing an answer might not arise immediately.

We close the sit by asking ourselves to listen to the body and let it be a guide. We give thanks for the miracle of our physical being and ask for strength, good health and well-being for all.

Metzora: Hidden and Revealed

There are many things we choose to keep hidden,
Experiences,
Dreams, thoughts and visions
We decide not to share.

And then there are times when we choose to shout out
What has happened
And describe the intricate patterns
Of our thoughts and experiences.

It is healthy and wise
To be discerning about
What to bring forth
And what to keep quiet and close to our souls.

There is also the inclination
To hide experiences of shame and embarrassment.
But these experiences fester when hidden,
Poisoning our bodies and souls.

Over time, shame can manifest in ways
That keeps us isolated and alone.

An antidote to shame
Is to come out of hiding
And speak what is so difficult to reveal.

When we are ready,
We do this with caution
With someone who is able to listen
With compassion and care.

Over time, revealing difficult feelings and experiences
Can help cleanse us
Of what has wreaked havoc on our bodies and souls.

Over time, these revelations
Can bring us back into relationship
With a deeper understanding of
Our own and
Each other's fragility and worth.

PRACTICE FOR THE WEEK

Non-Judgmental Awareness

We take our seats, rest the attention on the breath and set an intention to notice whatever arises in the mind with non-judgmental awareness. We will view whatever arises with interest and curiosity, avoiding self-criticism.

Watching the breath move through our bodies, we notice each time the mind wanders from the moment. As we notice a thought arising, a story breaking through, a feeling demanding attention, we label it as "thought," "story," or "feeling," and we bring the attention back to the breath.

With gentle strength, we choose to not follow the thought and we don't judge the feeling or ourselves for wandering. We give thanks for noticing and continue to return to the breath.

We do our best to view each thought, feeling or story that arises as an opportunity to practice non-judgmental awareness and return our attention to the moment.

We close the sit by giving thanks for what we noticed and by setting an intention that, as we go about our day, we will view our thoughts and experiences with curiosity and interest and without judgment.

Achrei Mot: After Death

After a death,
What is left?

Memories, stories,
Joys, pain,
Disappointments, delights,
A vast emptiness,
A taste of the mystery,
Eternity,
Forever.

After a death
We go on.
We must.
Life itself demands this.

And as we do,
Can we let rituals hold us,
Guide us,
Day to day,
Week to week,
As we make our way back into life?

Death is forever
And so is love.

We engage in rituals,
We take on practices,
So as to become spacious enough,
To mourn, to grieve, to cry,
To face the truth of death
And continue,
With all our hearts, souls and strength,
To love.

PRACTICE FOR THE WEEK

Calling on Eternal, Infinite Love

> We take our seats, bringing ourselves into an upright and
> awake posture.
> With gentleness and care, we rest the attention on the breath
> and set an intention to nourish our hearts and souls
> so we can better face the pain and joys of life.
>
> After a few moments, we say to ourselves this phrase from Psalms:
> *For your loving-kindness is before my eyes and I will walk*
> *in your truths.*   *Psalm 26:3*
>
> Over and over, we repeat this phrase, calling forth love that is
> infinite, eternal, love that holds us and gives us the strength
> to be present with difficult and painful truths.
> *For your loving-kindness is before my eyes and I will walk*
> *in your truths.*   *Psalm 26:3*
>
> We close the sit with the image of being held and filled with
> great abundant love.

Kedoshim: Holiness

Kidoshim tihyu. You shall be holy, the Infinite calls.
You shall be holy
Because I am holy,   Leviticus 19:1
Because all life is connected,
And everything you do matters.

You shall be holy
Because everything that ever happened
Created this very moment,
And everything that will ever be
Unfolds from here.

The experiences and choices
Of your Great, Great, Great, Great Grandparents
Whose names you do not know
Gave form to this life

And the choices,
Encounters,
Experiences and decisions
You make
Will shape generations you will never see.

You shall be holy
Because everything you do makes a difference
And all life unfolds from here.

Share what you have.
Treat all people with dignity.
Speak with intention and care.

Practice fairness,
Respect each other's differences,
Act for justice,
Seek forgiveness,
And love.

Love yourself.
Love each other.
Return to love again and again.

You shall be holy.
Live deeply into each moment,
And take the longest possible view.

Be holy
So that generations to come
Will say,
Let us give thanks for our ancestors
And for the beautiful world they left us.
Let us give thanks for their acts of holiness.
Let us give thanks for their love.

PRACTICE FOR THE WEEK

Sitting in Holiness

We seat ourselves in an awake posture, feeling where our
bodies make contact with our chairs or our cushions. We draw
our shoulders back so the heart space is open and notice the
sensations in our bodies as we take our seats.

We continue to call ourselves present by taking gentle, deep
breaths, feeling the vibrations as the breath moves in and out.
With kindness, we keep returning our attention to the movement
and sensations of the breath.

After a short while, we set an intention to hear the call:
Kidoshim tihyu, You shall be holy.

We feel this prayer as it travels on the breath
throughout the body:
Kidoshim tihyu, You shall be holy.

We do our best not to attach stories or thoughts to the call, returning again and again to the vibration of the words:

Kidoshim tihyu, You shall be holy.

Each time we notice the mind raising questions, doubts or objections, we give thanks for noticing and return to the breath and the words:
Kidoshim tihyu, You shall be holy.

This is a call and a promise. Each of us in our uniqueness, each of us as part of the magnificent unfolding of creation, shall be holy. We anchor our attention on this call:
Kidoshim tihyu, You shall be holy.

At the close of the sit, we give thanks and set our intentions for the day:

May I remember that I have the capacity to bring forth goodness and blessing. May my actions be for the benefit of all.

Emor: Speak

Here you are, the Mystery calls,
Here you are,
Right now.
This very moment is your life.

And this moment is perfect because
This is what is.

But the mind, never satisfied,
Seeks control,
Reaches for certainty,
Determined to fashion reality
According to its own image.

Let go, the Mystery implores.
Wonder, for awhile,
Not about changing the moment,
Wonder about changing
Your understanding,
Shifting your perspective,
So the energy spent
Bemoaning imperfection,
Clinging to regret,
And worrying about what will be
Can be put to better use.

Wonder about shifting your perspective,
Changing your understanding,
So you can step fully
Into what each moment offers,
What each moment asks.

The choice is yours.
Make a decision
About what attitudes,
What perspectives

You are going to encourage
In your mind, body and spirit.

This is not easy.
In this life there will always be loss,
There will always be things
That do not go the way we had hoped,
Expected or planned.

This is how it is,
And it is your choice
How you will meet each circumstance,
Each moment of your life.

Let the natural world be your guide.
Watch the spring come:
The flowers bloom,
Tiny buds bursting forth.

Feel spring stretch into summer:
The growing light,
The deepening green of trees.

And then watch summer turn to fall:
The leaves changing to orange, yellow, red, and brown
Before they let go
And drift back to earth.

As you sanctify these cycles
And place yourselves
Within this movement,
You will learn gratitude,
Courage and faith.
And you will learn to see the Mystery everywhere,
Present with you always,
From moment,
To moment,
To moment.

PRACTICE FOR THE WEEK

Meeting the Moment

We take our seats, coming to an upright and dignified posture, being aware of how and where we place our feet and hands. Pulling our shoulders slightly back so the heart space is open, we rest our attention on the breath, feeling the sensations as it moves in and through the body.

After a short while, we say with each breath:
I meet this moment fully, I meet it as a friend.

Into each thought, story or sensation
that passes through the mind, we say:
I meet this moment fully, I meet it as a friend.

When we notice fears, doubts, anxiety arise,
we return to the breath and say:
I meet this moment fully, I meet it as a friend.

To any dreams, hopes, yearnings
that claim our attention we say:
I meet this moment fully, I meet it as a friend.

With our attention returning again and again to the breath,
We watch as each moment passes into the next.
And to each moment, whatever it carries, we say:
I meet this moment fully, I meet it as a friend.

As we close our sit, we give thanks for each
moment and set an intention for the day:

I will meet this day fully.
And whatever this day brings,
I will meet it as a friend.

Behar: On the Mountain

The mist from Sinai travels down the valley.
We turn a corner and the mountain appears.
For a moment we can see its high peak,
Its craggy edges,
The rock faces sharp and smooth.

Then clouds drift in
And the mountain disappears.

But the memory remains:
A vision,
A hope,
A dream,
A knowing.

It is all One.
Everything,
Always.

Separation is an illusion.
There really is no us and them,
You and me.
There really is no "other."
It is all One.

And yet, here we are,
Each of us unique,
Each of us aware of distinction and separation.
And the understandable inclination that follows:
This is mine.
My money,
My home,
My food,
My property,
My resources,
My land.

What I have gathered,
What I have been blessed with,
What I have worked for
Is mine.

But the One responds:
Actually, everything is mine.
The earth is mine
And all that fills it,
All that arises from it,
All that dwells upon it,
Is mine.   *Psalm 24:1*

You are sojourners here,
Passing through this life,
You,
And all that is,
Is mine.   *Leviticus 25:23*

The soul knows this and yet,
In this life we get so attached.
We love,
We care,
We build,
We acquire.

Lift your eyes to the mountain, the One calls,
And remember:
Whatever you have acquired,
Whatever you have worked for,
Built,
Gathered,
Created,
Are gifts.

Yours to hold for a short while,
Yours to give away.

PRACTICE FOR THE WEEK
Receiving and Giving

We take our seats with awareness, and after settling into an awake and dignified posture, we rest our attention on the breath. We ask ourselves to notice the sensations and movement in the face, chest and stomach as the body receives the breath and as the body releases the breath back into the world.

After a short while, we set an intention to recognize each breath as a gift of the One and to release it with love. And we say gently to ourselves:

I receive this breath with gratitude. I release this breath with love.

When we notice our attention has wandered, we bring ourselves back by taking a slow, even, deep breath. We feel the breath move through us and say:
I receive this breath with gratitude. I release this breath with love.

We close the sit by giving thanks for the gift of breath that flows through all life.

Bechukotai: Rules for Alignment

There are rules to live by,
Statutes, laws.
Some we establish,
Others are a given,
Having been woven into the fabric of creation.

When we abuse the land,
Cut down forests,
Pollute the waters,
Dirty the skies,
There are consequences.

When we tear at each other's dignity,
Disregard need, inequality and desperation,
There are consequences.

All of our actions have impact.

Right action does not
Guarantee right results.
But seeking to do good,
Living with respect, reverence,
Dignity and care,
Keeps us in right relationship with each other
And aligned with the rhythms and harmonies of the earth.

Everything that has happened shaped this moment right now.
And all of our words, deeds and actions
Will shape the future for generations to come.

Let us step mindfully
As we make our way through this mysterious life,
For we walk in partnership with the Great Unfolding.

Here for a short time,
Our choices endure.

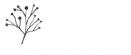

PRACTICE FOR THE WEEK
Calling Forth Harmony

We take our seats, and bring ourselves to an awake,
upright posture and we open our sit by saying a verse
from the final blessing in the *Amida*:
Sim shalom, tovah, uvracha, chayim,
chen, v'chesed, v'rachamim, aleynu.
Place peace, well-being, blessing, life,
grace, love and compassion upon us all.
We repeat the verse three times.

Drawing our shoulders back so the heart space is open, we set an
intention to invite a sense of harmony to flow in us and through us.

With gentleness and strength, we continue repeating the opening
phrase of the prayer:

Sim shalom, tovah, uvracha
Place peace, well-being and blessing upon us all.

Each time we notice the attention has wandered, we bring
ourselves back by returning to the breath and the rhythms and
vibrations of the prayer:

Sim shalom, tovah, uvracha
Place peace, well-being and blessing upon us all.

We close the sit by giving thanks for the gifts of creation and
saying aloud:

Sim shalom, tovah, uvracha, chayim,
chen, v'chesed, v'rachamim, aleynu
Place peace, well-being, blessing, life,
grace, love and compassion upon us all.

B'midbar
The Book of Numbers

B'midbar: In the Wilderness

The wilderness stretches before us.
And we step onto the unfolding path.

Within the exploration and discovery,
The Divine calls:

Take notice of whom you walk with,
Take notice of who is by your side.

Be aware of whom you can count on
And who can count on you.

Lift your eyes to the greater community
And see
Who among you are valued,
Who are counted,
And who are deemed unworthy of consideration.

Here in the wilderness of life's journey,
Let it be that we accept each other's frailties
And lift up each other's strengths.
Let it be that we honor each other's abilities
And allow for our failings and mistakes.
Let us see that this life is vast and deep
And there is a place for all of us.
There is enough need and opportunity
For everyone to be of use.

Let us enter the wilderness with this:
Everyone counts.
Everyone is of value.

Let us recognize the worth in ourselves and each other
And let this call to dignity and respect guide our way.

PRACTICE FOR THE WEEK

Everyone Matters

Taking our seats with awareness, and resting the attention on the breath, we set an intention to acknowledge that we live in an intricate web of connection and that everyone matters, everyone counts.

Engaging our imagination, we see and feel ourselves as part of an infinite web, connected to and a part of all. With each breath, we draw forth awareness of our connection to each other and the earth. Each breath reminds us that the web of connection is strong and true and we are here in relationship to all.

Each time we notice the mind has wandered, we take a slow, calm, even deep breath and open to the awareness of our interconnection with all.

At the close of the sit, we say:
Each of us is worthy. Each of us counts.
We are all here with each other.

Naso: What We Carry

Carry,
With great care,
The exquisite details
That life manifests,
The beauty
You discover, create and become.

Lift up what helps you.
Be aware of the sacred
That awakens you again and again
To the precious gifts of life.

Be mindful, also, of the brokenness
You carry,
The jealousy, rage and shame
That distorts your perceptions
And makes acceptable
What is absolutely deplorable.

Lift up and draw close to the sacred mystery of life's unfolding
By forging your own path
And dedicating yourself, for a time, to solitude.

Lift up and draw close to the sacred mystery of life's unfolding
By stepping forward, by joining in
And offering
The jewels of your heart.

Lift up holiness
And draw close
By revealing your treasures,
By declaring your brokenness
And letting your imperfections and your splendor be seen.

Could we possibly consider,
That with everything we carry,
With everything we are,

Glorious and flawed,
Magnificent and shattered,
We are blessed
And forever worthy of
This precious life?

PRACTICE FOR THE WEEK

Lifting Up Blessings

In this week's Torah portion, we hear the ancient blessing:

May the Infinite bless you and protect you,
May the Infinite's presence shine upon you with grace,
May the Infinite lift you up and place upon you peace.   Numbers 6:22-26

In this week's practice, we set an intention to receive this blessing, carry it with us and send it into the world.

Taking our seats, we read the blessing to ourselves three times. Then, closing our eyes, we bring awareness to the breath and its movement through the body.

After a few moments, we say gently to ourselves:

I am blessed and protected.
Grace and peace shine upon and through me.

We repeat this prayer over and over, returning to it whenever we notice the mind has wandered.

After a short time, we bring to mind people in our lives and say to each of them in turn:
You are blessed and protected.
Grace and peace shine upon and through you.

After a while we call to awareness aspects of nature:
Trees; birds; waters; sky; mountains. . . .
And say for each of them in turn:

You are blessed and protected.
Grace and peace shine upon and through you.

We close the sit by giving thanks and read through the ancient blessing once more with the intention of receiving it and carrying it with us.

Beha'altokha: Lifting Up the Lights

When we stood at Sinai,
You promised Your presence,
Your Torah,
Your strength.

And you asked for
Our commitment,
For us to remember and guard
The paths made known,
The wisdom revealed.

At Sinai the earth shook, the *shofar* wailed,
Everything disappeared,
And we were one with You, the Infinite Unfolding of All.

And then the world rushed back.
You donned your veil,
And we returned to the place
Where everything is distinct,
Where confusion reigns,
And where all that is
Will someday be no more.

Navigate this wilderness, you whispered,
You have everything you need.
The scroll of the book has been written upon you.   Psalm 40:8-9

Raise up the light,
Sound the trumpet,
And go forward.   Numbers 8:2, 10:2

If only it were that easy.
This being human is so complex.
Regret, doubt and fear
Arise and produce cravings that masquerade as truth.
And we go astray
And get lost again and again.

I am here, the Divine calls.
I am so close.
I am in the clouds of confusion
And I am in the clarity of vision.

Look for me.
Watch for me.

In clouds and in fire,
With subtle signs
And extraordinary visions,
I will guide you.

And even as you get lost
Led astray by thoughts, circumstances and fears,
I will continue to shine.

And I will remind you with my Presence
That there will always be opportunities
To return to the path.

I will lift up lights to remind you that
No matter how far away you are,
How lost, how unsure, how broken,
I will help you return to presence.
I will help you find your way.

Confusion and clarity will arise and pass.
Peace will come,
As will contention.
The path forward will appear and then fade from view.

And through all of it I am with you.
Even as confusion reigns,
And fear and doubt persist,
I will lift up my lights
And illuminate the way.

PRACTICE FOR THE WEEK

Lifting Up the Lights

Taking our seats, and resting the attention on the breath, we set an intention to be aware that a sacred light resides in each of us and flows through all the world. A sacred light shines in each being, in all life.

Sitting, aware of the sensation of being held by our chairs or cushions, we imagine and feel the sacred light inside of us, locating it in our bodies, tending it with the breath. With each breath, we touch the light and notice its contours, colors and movements. With each breath, we take note that this sacred light that is within us also flows though all creation. We continue to touch and sense the light with our awareness.

Each time we notice our attention has strayed, we return to the breath and the sensations of the sacred light moving within and through us.

At the close of the sit, with gentleness and love, we say to ourselves, *This light is always here to guide me.*

Shelach Lecha: Send Forth Yourself

Shelach Lecha –
Send yourself forth.

The unknown awaits you,
New lands to be discovered,
New ways of being
That are promised,
Hoped for,
Imagined.

Shelach Lecha –
Send yourself forth.
There are so many beginnings awaiting your arrival.

Yes, the soul says, I will go.
I will step forward in new ways.
I will see with new eyes.
I will explore what can be different, exciting, promising, possible.
Yes, I will go.
There is so much to be discovered,
So much to be enjoyed.

But one step forward and the mind begins to spin:
You can't do this.
You don't have the tools, the insights, the imagination
To change, to grow,
To become.

Go back to being tiny, to being small.
Go back to the narrow place.

The Mystery calls:
Notice that when fears take hold,
The mind constricts and vision narrows.
And the thoughts
That inspire doubt and
Insist on fear
Are perceived as the only truths.

In moments of spaciousness,
When our perspective expands,
It is possible to see that much of the fear and doubt
Are only stories that the mind has conjured.

How to return to a spacious perspective?
How to discern illusion and truth?

The call from the Mystery rings like a bell:
Practice.
Do *Mitzvot.* Engage in acts of connection.

Give thanks.
Acknowledge beauty.
Respond with compassion.
Offer help.
Seek guidance.
Listen well.
Engage with ritual.
Do acts of justice.
Speak words of blessing.

Engaging in these actions will help expand our perspectives,
And deepen our discernment
So we can better see
What is most true.

Shelach Lecha – Send yourself forth, the Mystery calls,
Expansive possibilities await your arrival.

PRACTICE FOR THE WEEK
Spacious Perspective

We take our seats and let the attention rest on the breath,
following the breath into all parts of the body: neck, shoulders,
arms, hands, face, torso, legs and feet. As we notice places that
feel tense or tight, we breathe gently into these areas.

After a few minutes, we set an intention to hold whatever arises in the mind in spaciousness.

As a thought arises, we name it as a thought and breathe into it with gentleness and watch it pass. We take notice of thoughts that cause a constriction in the body or stir up tense emotions and send a calm soothing breath into the thoughts and into any tightness or constriction. Over and over again, we imagine the breath as a soft breeze creating spaciousness around each thought, story or image.

When thoughts arise that bring fear, doubt or worries that feel so vast there seems to be nothing else, we breathe gentleness and love into the whole body, doing our best to return the attention to the breath again and again.

We close the sit by offering gratitude and setting an intention to see and name the beauty and the blessings the day brings forth.

Korach

As our ancestors wandered in the wilderness,
Seeking their way,
Korach, a Levite and respected authority,
Rose up and grasped for power.

Challenging Moses' leadership, he declared:

The entire community is holy,
The One is within us all,
No one should be raised above anyone else.   Numbers 16:3

And even though his words held truth,
They could not be received
Because *Korach* himself could not live what he was speaking.

Perhaps it was ambition, envy, insecurity or greed,
That encouraged *Korach* to rebel
And grab for power.
Perhaps it was sadness, suffering, pain or fear
That caused him to speak for communal well-being
While attempting to take for himself what he claimed was for all.

Whatever his motivation,
This grasping for power,
Could not stand.
The earth itself would not let it be.

As *Korach* stood and made his claim,
The desert floor opened and swallowed him.
Korach — and his family, who had followed his lead —
Were swallowed by the earth
Alive
And Whole.

And they stayed underground
And lived and grew.

And then, deep from within the living, breathing, abundant earth
Korach and his children began to sing:
They sang of the sacred and a longing for the One.

They sang:
Rebel for the sake of communal well-being.
Challenge authority
For the sake of love, peace, truth and justice.

The songs of the children of *Korach*
Are wisdom echoed from the earth
And each note calls us back into connection
With each other
And the Infinite One.

Songs from the *Children of Korach*:*

My heart is astir with a good thing.   Psalm 45:2

The One is our refuge and strength,
Our help in times of trouble,
Very close.   Psalm 46:1-2

Fulfilled are those who know
That in each moment
The One dwells within us
And in each moment
We dwell within the One.   Psalm 84:5

Joyful are those who trust in the One.   Psalm 84:13

Singing and dancing, we declare:
Everything springs from the One.   Psalm 87:7

Let me hear what the One will say,
The One will speak of well-being for all.   Psalm 85:9

---

* Twelve (some say eleven) of the 150 psalms are attributed to "The Children of *Korach*": Psalms 42-49, 85, 87, 88. There is disagreement about whether psalm 43 should be included. Though it does not say *The Children of Korach*, it is believed to be literarily joined to the preceding psalm.

Love and Truth meet
Peace and Justice embrace.

Truth springs forth from the earth,
And justice looks down from the heavens. *Psalm 85:11-12*

PRACTICE FOR THE WEEK
Listening to the *Songs of the Children of Korach*

We take our seats with intention, settling into an awake posture and letting our attention rest on the breath. Slowly, we read through the verses of the *Songs of the Children of Korach* three times, breathing them into our bodies, noticing how the phrases feel inside. Each day we take notice of what phrases resonate and which ones feel more distant.

When we notice a phrase that feels good in our bodies, we repeat it over and over again to ourselves, letting the song calm and soothe our souls. We can do this with one word, a part of a phrase or we can put different verses together.

As we become aware that our attention has wandered, we bring ourselves back by returning to the breath and to the words of the song.

If no part of the song sounds true for us, we can let our attention follow the Breath of All Life, moving through us and out into the world.

At the end of our sit, we offer gratitude and set an intention to notice the melodies of the world that we hear as we go about our day. If we have found a verse, a phrase or a word that resonates for us, we carry it with us during the day and return to it as a way to bring us back to awareness and back to center.

Chukat: Statutes

The Torah reminds us that
At some point
Each of us will die.
That is for sure.

But how we engage with the waters of life
Is an open question.

How will we meet beauty and wonder?
How will we face disappointment and pain?
What will we do with the mistakes we have made?
Where will we find and create solace, comfort and love?

Take on practices, the Torah pleads.
Set intentions. Make commitments.
Let these draw you into the waters
And help you navigate your way.

Place before your eyes the intention to see blessings,
To notice the good.

Let your mouth speak words of gratitude and praise.

Don't duck from pain.
Don't run from grief.
Stop and feel loss
And heartbreak.
Allow wounds to be wounds
And slowly to heal.

Acknowledge mistakes.
Let these experiences speak
And be teachers and guides.

The waters of life are in constant motion.
And everything passes, changes, becomes something else.

Joy, sadness, love, pain,

Everything passes, changes, becomes something else.

May practice and devotion hold us steady.
And may the dance of the waters
Inspire our songs.

Spring up from the well, waters of life. We sing to waters, to the Source of all.
Numbers 21:17

PRACTICE FOR THE WEEK
Opening to the *Mayim Chayim*, the Waters of Life

We take our seats with awareness, positioning ourselves in an awake, upright posture. Focusing on the breath, feeling the sensations as the breath moves through the body, we call ourselves to attention.

After a short while, we begin to repeat the phrase *Mayim Chayim*, Waters of Life. Letting this phrase travel on the breath, we feel its rhythm and vibration. *Mayim Chayim*, Waters of Life.

Each time we notice a thought arise, we say, *Mayim Chayim* and invite the thought to dissolve into the waters of life.

Continuing to repeat the phrase, letting it travel with the breath, we begin to imagine feeling the living waters move through us, offering cleansing and clarity. And we can imagine the waters surrounding us, holding us with care.

At the close of the sit, we offer this prayer:

May we draw water in joy from the living well   *Isaiah 12:3*

Balak

God uncovered Balaam's eyes and Balaam saw a messenger of the Divine standing right there on the path.   Numbers 22:31

We so often go on our way,
Seeing what we expect,
Perceiving what we assume.
So much of what we notice is determined by habit and routine.

Sometimes we need to lose our way,
To walk into walls,
To fall to the ground,
In order to free our gaze.

Sometimes it is a messenger who awakens us.
Coming forward with understanding and insight,
She helps us rediscover the path.

And sometimes the messengers are more hidden.
Disguised as turmoil,
Pain,
Frustration,
Fear,
They too come to awaken us
And call us forward.
They too come to unveil our eyes
So we can see,
Speak,
And live
What is true.

Who are the messengers on our paths?
What is it they are here to teach?
And how do we discern their guidance?

Sometimes we need to lose our way,
To walk into walls,
To fall to the ground
In order to free our gaze.

We need to return again and again and again
To prayer,
To practice,
To each other,
To find the courage and willingness to see.
For the One yearns to be revealed
And messengers are standing at the ready
To guide us and show us the way.

Let us recognize moments when
We hear the mystery speak,
And humbled, with eyes unveiled,
We behold visions from beyond.   *Numbers 24:4*

These visions linger long after the clarity dissolves.
They become other messengers on the path,
Pushing and prodding us
To See,
Speak,
And live
What is true.

PRACTICE FOR THE WEEK

Seeing

As we take our seats, we acknowledge that stories, thoughts and emotions that arise before our eyes can become the lenses through which we perceive our experiences. When fear arises, the world looks one way and when joy, sadness, hope or pain arises, the world takes on different hues. Stories and expectations can distort what is actual and true in the moment.

As we sit and rest our attention on the breath, we watch as thoughts arise in the mind. They may be thoughts that stir an emotional response that can be felt in the body. We may notice familiar stories about the past as well as dreams or anxiety about the future.

Each time we notice a thought, story or emotion arise, we do our best to name it as such, saying gently to ourselves:

This is a thought that brings worry, fear, hope.
This is my mind circling the past.
This is my mind yearning to predict what the future will bring.
This is a story of sadness, of frustration.
This is a story that stirs doubt.

Each time we name a thought, story or feeling, we return our attention to the breath, letting it bring a soothing calm.

At the end of the sit, we give thanks for all we perceived and we set an intention to notice with love and patience the stories, habits and expectations that arise and cloud our vision.

Pinchas

Mindful of the mysterious unfolding of life,
And seeing that his days would soon reach their end,
Moses called God by a new name:
Elohai haruchot l'chol basar
Source of the Spirits of all Flesh.   *Numbers 27:15-16*

Aware that he had been led on paths unexpected,
Carrying a people who were reluctant, lost and afraid,
Moses called on the Infinite:
Elohai haruchot l'chol basar
Source of the Spirits of all Flesh.

Seeing his mistakes,
Bearing his responsibilities,
Moses called on the One who had called on him:
Elohai haruchot l'chol basar
Source of the Spirits of all Flesh.

Looking back at the journey,
The visions that had been lifted up,
The structures and statutes that had been carefully laid down,
Moses called on his Intimate Companion:
Elohai haruchot l'chol basar
Source of the Spirits of all Flesh:

When my flesh is no longer filled with Your spirit
And this body has reached its end,
Who shall follow in my wake?
What do I leave behind?

Take Joshua, the One answered,
For he is filled with spirit.
His vision is clear and he is not bound by fear.
Before the entire community,
Lay your hands upon his shoulders,
And from your radiance
Bestow upon him awareness, presence and humility.

So the people will be able to hear his voice
And follow his command.

Numbers 27:18-20

Elohai haruchot l'chol basar
Source of the Spirits of all Flesh,
Help us remember we are flesh and spirit,
Vulnerable and strong,
Here for our little while,
Doing our best to navigate this wilderness of life.

Elohai haruchot l'chol basar
Source of the Spirits of all Flesh,
Lead us gently on paths unknown.
Help us see with eyes of forgiveness.
Help us recognize what is ours to do.
Help us weave lives of meaning
And pass on generously all we have learned.

Elohai haruchot l'chol basar
Source of the Spirits of all Flesh
May the radiance of your presence fill us,
Now, and for the length of our days.

PRACTICE FOR THE WEEK

Welcoming the Spirit

We take our seats and rest our attention on the breath. Following
the breath as it moves through the body, we draw our shoulders
back, place our hands in a way that keeps the heart space open,
and take notice of how it feels to be grounded in our chairs or on
our cushions.

After a short while, we call on the name of God:
Elohai haruchot l'chol basar
Source of the Spirits of all Flesh

We let this name travel on the breath, feeling the Spirits of all Life fill our bodies, reaching into every crevice, massaging each organ, traveling along veins and arteries. With each breath, we watch the Spirit of All Life fill us and pour through us into the world.

When we notice that our minds have wandered,
we return our attention to the breath:
Elohai haruchot l'chol basar
Source of the Spirits of all Flesh

We close the sit by giving thanks and setting an intention for how we would like to enter the day.

Mattot: Tribes

There are times when battles rage,
When vengeance rules,
When terror reigns,
And cruelty triumphs.

There are times when we so lose touch
With the essence of all that is
That we lash out and do harm
Feeling that this is our right.

Each of us struggles.
Each of us battles.
Each of us has places inside
Where shame, fear, regret, betrayal, humiliation
Have done violence to our souls.

Our willingness to confront these demons
Begins to relieve them of their power.
Our willingness to acknowledge the battles
Lessens the fury they unleash.

We are all members of a tribe,
Of a country, a community, a family,
And we are all creatures of earth,
Manifestations of the cosmos.

A glimpse from a wider perspective,
Where distinctions disappear
And we can see,
Just for a moment, that we are all here together,
Can help us lay down some of the narratives
That cause us to defend and destroy.

We are all here together,
Hugely important
And fleeting specks of dust.

May mercy reign.
May compassion rule.
May peace triumph.

PRACTICE FOR THE WEEK

Soothing Calming Waters

We take our seats with awareness and bring attention to the movement of the breath.

We acknowledge that there are battles that rise within each of us and at times cause us to do harm.

We set an intention to bring a sense of calm into our hearts, bodies and minds, to ease some of the struggles and help us discern more peaceful and skillful ways to deal with the battles that arise.

Taking slow, calm, even deep breaths, we begin to imagine the breath as soothing, calming waters that flow through us gently, with ease. It might be helpful to see the color of the water, to feel its temperature and follow its motion as it moves through each part of our bodies, soothing, calming water flowing through us gently, with ease.

Each time we notice the attention has wandered, that demons are rising, or thoughts are threatening to do battle, we return the attention to the breath and the soothing calming waters.

At the close of the sit, we give thanks and set an intention that as we go about our day we will notice when the inclination to do battle arises and we will meet these thoughts and inclinations with slow and calming deep breaths.

Massei: Journeys

As the book of Numbers comes to a close,
We listen as our ancestors recount their wanderings:

The journey began
With slavery in Egypt,
Giving way to the vast desert wilderness
And the possibilities and challenges of freedom.

On their way, our ancestors got lost.
They stumbled,
They wailed and wept,
As they sought to discover
How they should live and
Who they could be.

In the rawness of the wilderness,
They experienced their own cruelty,
The harshness that can result from fear, shame and loss,
The brutality that seeks to destroy what is different,
And what it cannot understand.

Over and over again, our ancestors
Battled with themselves and each other,
Trying to find ways out of disappointment, anger and pain.

There is no way out but through, the Holy One calls,
And you can take only one step at a time.

Gather together,
Act with honesty,
And acknowledge your truths.

The path will wind continuously through light and shadow
And it is your task to continually return
To walking with dignity, integrity and grace.

PRACTICE FOR THE WEEK

Light and Shadow

We take our seats with awareness and settle into an upright and awake posture. Resting the attention on the breath, we notice the breath moving through the body, reaching down the torso, arms and legs. We feel the breath moving into the shoulders neck, head and face.

After a short while, we feel and see the breath as light – a soft, graceful light that fills our bodies and travels in and through us. With each in-breath, the light enters. And with each out-breath, the light moves gently out into the world.

When we notice a thought or story arise, casting a shadow on the light, we acknowledge it and gently bring our attention back to the breath and the light filling and flowing through us.

Over and over again, as we notice our minds have wandered, we return our awareness to the light traveling on the breath.

As we close the sit, we give thanks for everything on our journey that brought us to this moment and we set an intention to walk into the day with dignity and grace.

D'varim

The Book of Deuteronomy

D'varim: Words

These are the words.   *Deuteronomy 1:1*

These are the words that describe our journey to this moment.
These are the words that lay the foundation for the journeys ahead.

The fifth book of the Torah begins by reminding us
Of the power of our words and the impact of our stories.

Who we have been,
And who we will continue to become,
Is fashioned through the narratives we weave.

How do we speak of the moments when we have missed the mark,
When we have done something we later regret?

What do we say of those times when we were lost and afraid,
And, constricted by doubt,
Caused pain to each other and ourselves?

How do we recount our joys and successes?
In what ways do we speak of our experiences
Of connection, awareness and love?

Our paths are shaped by the stories we tell.

Some of our stories remind us of our strengths.
They encourage our awareness
And call forth our commitment to reach for our best, most glorious selves.
Other stories underline our shortcomings
And encourage us to feel small, afraid and unable to change.

Some of our words inspire doubt,
Others generate hope and faith.
Some of our narratives insist on regret
While others offer forgiveness, understanding and love.

Our experiences are what they are.
The stories are ours to weave and tell.

PRACTICE FOR THE WEEK

These are the Words

As we take our seats each day this week, we center ourselves by resting the attention on the breath. We follow the breath through the body and let it anchor us on our seats or cushions. We notice how it feels to be held in our place and we let the breath guide us in being attentive to the moment.

After a short while, we ask for a word or phrase to arise that we can place upon our hearts and before our eyes. The intention is not to busy the mind but to ask with interest and curiosity what word or phrase could help call us present and guide us into each moment.

What word or phrase could direct our attention in a way that would be helpful?

We make this request with gentleness and notice how it feels.

When and if a word or phrase appears, we place it upon our hearts by repeating it to ourselves again and again, letting it travel on the breath. Each time we notice our attention has wandered, we call ourselves back by returning our awareness to the word or phrase. If a word or phrase does not arise easily, we can let the request go and continue to anchor our attention on the breath.

Va'etchanan: Graced

Upon the mountain,
In the midst of fire,
The Infinite One spoke to each of us,
To all of us,
Panim b'Panim – face *within* face.   *Deuteronomy 5:4*

We were completely revealed,
And, afraid of the intimacy,
Of the directness of the call,
We placed hesitation, doubt and fear
Between ourselves and the One.

But the fire blazed,
And the One would not be deterred.
Deep within our beings,
Upon our hearts, minds and souls,
The One engraved our Torah, our truths.

There are moments when awareness fills our bodies.
Torah shines from our eyes
And comes forth through our lives.
Other times, we forget wisdom is present
And we get lost in clouds of confusion and fear.

The scroll of the book is written upon you,
The One calls,
Everything you need,
Has been placed in your core.   *Psalm 40:8-9*

Shema: Listen. Pay attention.
It will help you remember
The One.
It will help you return
To the teachings and truths of your soul.

Shema, Ve'ahafta   *Deuteronomy 6:4-9*
Listen. Pay attention
And you will learn to respond
To all that life brings with love.

Upon the mountain,
In the midst of the fire,
The one spoke to each of us *panim b'panim*,
Placing within us wisdom and guidance
For this journey through life.

And upon the mountain,
In the midst of the fire,
The one spoke to all of us *panim b'panim*,
Placing within us the awareness
That we are here
To love.

Shema, Ve'ahafta
Listen. Pay attention,
And as you walk through life
You will love,
With all your heart,
With all your soul
And with all your strength.   *Deuteronomy 6:4-9*

Ken yihi ratzon. May it be so.

PRACTICE FOR THE WEEK

Shema

We take our seats and bring our attention to the breath. We call
ourselves present by taking notice of the movement of the body
as it receives a breath and as it releases a breath.

After a few moments, we call out the *Shema* three times, feeling
the vibration of the prayer in our bodies.

Shema Yisrael Adonai Eloheynu Adonai Echad
Listen, all those who wrestle, the Infinite Unfolding, diverse and distinct, the Infinite Unfolding is one.

Then we take the call *Shema, Ve'ahafta* and place it upon our hearts by repeating it over and over: *Shema, Ve'ahafta* Listen and Love. Each time we notice the mind has wandered, we bring the attention back by returning to the call: *Shema, Ve'ahafta* Listen and Love.

We close the sit by calling out the *Shema* again and setting our intention for the day:
May I listen well.
May I respond to myself and others with love.

Ekev: Because

Because.
Because everything is connected,
Because everything follows on the heels of something else,
Because every action has consequences beyond anything we will ever know:
> *Pay attention.*
> *Be mindful of the path.*
> *Walk with awe.*   Deuteronomy 8:6

Because we can forget we are not all powerful,
Because we can forget we are not the source,
Because we can forget that life is a precious and fragile gift:
> *Let the heart and soul be nourished.*
> *Savor the fullness and be satisfied with the richness of each moment.*
> *Pause and give thanks.*   Deuteronomy 8:10

Because it is easy to go astray,
To get lost in anger, fear and doubt:
> *Love the stranger*   Deuteronomy 10:19

Love yourself even when you are not at your best.
Love others even when they disappoint or fall short.

Because we can set intentions,
Because we can act with dignity, awareness and grace
And still cannot predict how life will unfold:
> *Cultivate awe.*
> *Be discerning.*
> *Walk with integrity.*   Deuteronomy 10:12

Because we are connected to each other,
Because we are connected to all creatures
And to all the earth,
Because everything we do matters,
And every action makes a difference:
> *Listen well.*
> *Love fully.*
> *Be of service.*
> *And direct the stirrings of your heart,*
> *And the offerings of your soul*
> *To bring benefit and blessing to all.*   Deuteronomy 10:12, 11:13

PRACTICE FOR THE WEEK

Fullness and Satisfaction

We take our seats, settling into an awake and upright posture. We bring our attention to the breath, noticing its shape and sensations as it moves throughout the body. To guide our concentration, we might see the breath as a color, one that might change or stay the same as it comes into the body and flows back out into the world.

After a short while, we set an intention to receive each breath as a gift, and we say to ourselves:
Each breath is a gift. In its fullness is everything I need.

Over and over again, we repeat to ourselves:
Each breath is a gift. In its fullness is everything I need.

We take notice of any resistance that arises, any stories, thoughts or feelings that challenge the thought that:
This breath is a gift. In its fullness is everything I need
And we breathe gently into these thoughts.

Each time we notice the attention has wandered, we give thanks for noticing, kindly tell ourselves we do not need to give our attention to these thoughts right now and return the attention to the breath, saying to ourselves:
Each breath is a gift. In its fullness is everything I need.

Toward the end of our sit, we take 3-5 minutes for gratitude, articulating for ourselves what it is we feel grateful for.
Gently, with love we say:
I am grateful for . . .
I am grateful for . . .
I am grateful for . . .

We close the sit by saying again:
Each breath is a gift. In its fullness is everything I need.

Re'eh: See

In preparation for their journey across the river,
To the land they had been promised,
Our ancestors were told:

See.
Every day you will have a choice.
Every day you will choose what you will notice,
And what you allow to guide your way.
Every day you will decide how to respond to a multitude of encounters
And how you will define each of your experiences.

See. Pay attention:
Notice your expectations.
When do they propel you forward?
And when do they bind you?

Notice your reactions when you feel challenged,
And what you do when faced with conflict and pain.

Be aware of your responses when faced with disagreements
And are confronted by ideas and experiences you find unsettling.

Notice where you feel comfortable,
And in what circumstances you feel safe.

For you are preparing to cross the river
To a land that is completely unknown.

It will lead you on new terrain
And ask you to continually define your path.

Thoughts will arise to scare you,
And might cause you to lash out or hide.

Thoughts will arise to confound you,
And could cause you, at times, to lose your way.

And insights will arise to guide you
And help you discern what is true.

Every day, new terrain opens before us
And we have to decide how to proceed.

Nurture yourself with practice, the Torah calls.
Be mindful of what you take into your body
And notice where the thoughts and stories of the mind lead.

For every day new terrain opens before us
And we choose how we will walk,
And what we will see.

PRACTICE FOR THE WEEK

Noticing

We take our seats with awareness and settle into an awake posture. Resting the attention on the breath, we bring ourselves present.

After a short while, we invite this visualization:

We imagine ourselves sitting on the banks of a river watching the water flow. We feel the ground underneath us and see and smell the water. We notice the water's color and the patterns it makes as it moves.

Grounded on the earth, we set an intention that each time a thought appears or a story arises we will send it into the river and let it flow away. Every thought, every story, is placed into the waters and we watch as each fades, becoming part of the river itself.

When we notice our minds have wandered and we are traveling with our thoughts down the river, we gently call ourselves back, reposition ourselves on the earth and let our thoughts flow into the waters.

As we close our sit, we express gratitude and ask for the wisdom to see clearly and make wise choices as we go about the day.

Shoftim: Wise Judgment

Justice, Justice shall you pursue.   Deuteronomy 19:9

Through words and actions,
Awareness and perception,
Through balance and fortitude
Discipline and strength,
Cultivate discernment.

Notice when you are being a harsh judge,
When criticism of yourself and others
Causes unwise thoughts and actions to arise.
Practice noticing with gentle awareness,
Realizing this is an inclination in everyone.
Return again and again to compassion
For yourself and others.
Consider that everyone is doing the best they can in each moment.

Notice the ways you use your power
And display your strength.
Notice when you grasp and seek control
And have to be better than anyone else.
Return again and again to humility,
Remembering you are a channel, not the source,
And your strengths, blessings, insights and power
Are gifts to be offered for the benefit of all.

Notice how you are called to be of service
And what inspires you to make that offering
Or retreat and turn away.
Explore what is true for you to give
And what needs to stay close to your own heart and soul.

Remember the power of words.
Be mindful of your speech.
Listen well to others.
Be discerning in what you do and say.

And seek Me, the Mystery calls,
Return to me again and again.
Align your body, mind, heart and soul with me
And walk in the ways of love.   *Deuteronomy 19:9*

PRACTICE FOR THE WEEK

Noticing

We take our seats with awareness and, resting the attention
on the breath, we place this intention on our hearts and minds:
I will see clearly and act wisely.

We repeat this phrase over and over, letting it travel with the breath:
I will see clearly and act wisely.

Each time we notice our attention has wandered, or thoughts
rise up to challenge or judge this assertion, with strength and
discipline, we return our attention to the breath and to our intent:
I will see clearly and act wisely.

We close the sit with a few calm, even deep breaths and with the
intention that, as we go about our day, we will notice when harsh
judgments arise and begin to shape our words, thoughts and
actions. As we notice, we will do our best to soften the judgments
with awareness and compassion.

Ki Tetze: As You Go Out

Go out, the Torah calls,
Face what is difficult,
What is problematic and harsh.
Face what you fear,
Look at the shame, guilt and hatred within you.

Notice the raging inside
And what causes you to lash out.
Notice the battles you seek
And the battles that seek and find you.

But who wants to really look
At all this confusion and pain?
Who wants to confront so much anguish
And fear?

There is no way out but through, the Holy One calls.
Go out and acknowledge the conflicts you encounter
And the disputes you create.

And remember,
The harsh voices
That insist on shame,
On fear,
On guilt,
Live inside each of us.

Each of us struggles
As these demons battle and rage.

Go out and see yourself in each other.
Look for commonalities, for connections.
Seek to care.

And remember that pain
Is best met with tenderness,
And the inclination to do battle
Is softened as we turn toward
Forgiveness, compassion and love.

PRACTICE FOR THE WEEK

Compassion

Through a compassion meditation, we seek to turn our hearts and minds toward love and kindness.

We take our seats, settle into an awake posture and rest the attention on the breath.

After a few minutes of noticing the sensations of the breath moving through our bodies, we begin by offering a blessing to ourselves.

Gently, we acknowledge our beauty and fragility and say to ourselves three times:

May I be blessed with love.
May I be blessed with peace.
May I be blessed with well-being.

We then turn our attention to someone whom we love easily.
We see them in our minds and hearts and say to them three times:

May you be blessed with love.
May you be blessed with peace.
May you be blessed with well-being.

Then we bring to mind someone with whom there is some pain, some need for healing, not the most difficult person in our lives, just someone with whom there has been a small rift. And to them we say three times:

May you be blessed with love.
May you be blessed with peace.
May you be blessed with well-being.

Throughout our sit, we continue to invite more people into our hearts and minds and say these blessings for each of them.
We take notice of who arrives to receive a blessing and how it feels to focus our attention on each person. We might have an

experience in which a person arises in our hearts/minds and our inclination is to not want to offer them a blessing. When this happens, it is important to make a compassionate choice. Sometimes it is OK to let a person go, knowing there will be another time when we can more freely offer them a blessing.

We close the sit by saying:
May all beings be blessed with love,
May all beings be blessed with peace,
May all beings be blessed with well-being.

We set the following intention:
As I go about the day, I will respond to myself and the people I encounter with compassion and kindness.

Ki Tavo: As You Enter

As we stand on the threshold of a new year,
Preparing ourselves to enter,
Tradition offers
Guidance for the journey.

Ki Tavo—As you enter—
As you enter a new place,
As you enter a new moment,
Take time to recall the journey.

Remember the experiences that challenged your soul,
That tore at your heart
And caused you to struggle with sadness and pain.

Remember the experiences of joy and celebration,
Moments of love and gratitude,
Deeds of connection,
Sparks of insight.

Take notice of what you have discovered
And who you have become.

And from these fruits of experiences and encounters,
Make an offering.
Let it come from the fullness of yourself.
And as you do, say these words:
Here I am.
I have come. I have entered.
Here I am, now.   *Deuteronomy 26:10*

As you enter,
Practice silence
And listen,
For in this very moment,
And in this very moment,
And in this very moment,
You are becoming a people
In relationship with the Mysterious Unfolding of All Life.   *Deuteronomy 27:9*

As we enter a new place,
As we enter a New Year,
May we unburden ourselves of harsh criticism and judgment.
May we give thanks for everything that brought us to this moment,
And may we declare our willingness to make an offering of all that
has grown
And all we have gathered.
For we are here in relationship with the Mysterious Unfolding of All Life.

Blessed may we be as we enter and blessed may we be as we go forth.

Deuteronomy 28:6

PRACTICE FOR THE WEEK

Calling Ourselves Present

As we take our seats, we acknowledge we are on the threshold of
the New Year. Following the breath into the chest, neck, face and
head, along the shoulders and back and down the arms, torso and
legs, we settle ourselves in our seats.

After a few minutes, we give thanks for the journey
of this past year and say to ourselves:
Here I am, now.

We acknowledge we are standing on the threshold
of what will be and we say:
Here I am, now.

We let this phrase travel on the breath,
throughout the whole body, repeating again and again:
Here I am, now.

When we notice our attention has shifted to thoughts
and stories connected to the past, with kindness,
we call ourselves back to the moment:
Here I am, now.

When we notice we are thinking about what will be
in the future, with gentleness, we return to the moment:
Here I am, now.

Each time we notice the attention has wandered,
we bring ourselves back with the call:
Here I am, now.

As we close the sit, we set the following intentions:
When we devote time to reviewing the past year,
we will do so with love and kindness.

We will give voice to our gratitude. We will acknowledge the
blessings we have experienced and the good we have done.

Blessed may we be as we enter and
Blessed may we be as we go forth.   *Deuteronomy 28:6*

Nitzavim: Standing Here

We stand here today.

We stand here today with all those we love,
With all those with whom we joyfully share this passage through life.

And we stand here today with all those we have been taught to call other,
And those we have learned to demonize and hate.

We stand here today with all those who came before us,
The generations upon whose shoulders we stand.

And we stand here today with all who will come after us:
Our children's, children's, children's children,
Who will someday call us ancestor.

We stand here today to enter into a covenant
To live in harmony with each other
And all the world.

We gather to step across boundaries of fear, anger and pain,
To ease our inclinations toward contention
And to release our need to always be right.

We gather to make a commitment
To love,
To act with kindness,
To seek understanding,
To offer forgiveness,
To be of service.

We gather to make a commitment to see the Divine in all.

This is not too much for you, the One declares.
It is not beyond your capacity.
It is not beyond your reach.
All this is very close to you.
It is in your mouth and in your heart to do.   Deuteronomy 30:14

Choose life.   *Deuteronomy 30:19*
Choose relationship.
Choose to return again and again to being loving and kind.
This is not too much for you.
It is in your mouth and in your heart to do.

We stand here today,
All of us together,
On the threshold of a New Year.

May we inspire each other to live with compassion and awareness,
To make choices that bring forth forgiveness and love.

And may our words and deeds unfold in such a way
That our children's, children's, children's children will say:
Let us give thanks for our ancestors
And let us give thanks for this beautiful, love-filled world they have left
in their wake.

PRACTICE FOR THE WEEK

Awareness

Taking our seats with dignity and following the breath into all parts
of the body, we locate ourselves and say *Hineni* — Here I am.

Feeling ourselves on our chairs or cushions, held by the wondrous
and nourishing earth, we say: *Hineni* — Here I am.

We then direct our attention to ourselves in relationship with all
life, remembering that we are connected to the land, waters, trees,
birds, mountains, animals and sky, and we say *Hinenu* — Here we
are. Over and over we repeat, *Hinenu* — Here we are.

After a short while, we open our attention to sense our
interdependent relationship with all people — with those we love
and with those whom we have labeled enemy or "other" and
we say: *Hinenu* — Here we are.

Continuing to follow the breath moving through our bodies,
the breath of all life that moves through all, we say
Hinenu — Here *we* are.

Whenever we notice our attention has wandered and we have
drifted away, we give thanks for noticing and we give thanks
for the opportunity to do *teshuvah*, to return to the moment
and to the awareness of our interconnection with all life.
Hinenu — Here *we* are.

At the close of the sit, we give thanks for gifts of this past year
and we set an intention to act with kindness and love
for the benefit of all.

Vayelech: As We Go

Again, we turn to cross over
Into new beginnings.

Be strong and courageous,
The Torah calls,
Even as the road is challenging,
Even as there are situations to fear.

Be strong and courageous.
Walk with the ancestors.
Walk with each other.
Walk with the One.

Be strong and courageous
Because it is so easy to get lost,
To go astray,
To forget what is important and true.

Be mindful of what you bring forth with your words and actions.
Don't let fear guide you.

And search for and discover the songs of your souls,
The true songs,
The reverent songs.
The songs that speak of love and connection
And remind us we are here to bring blessing.

Sing these songs to yourself.
Sing these songs to each other.
Teach these songs to your children.

And when the road gets narrow,
And adversaries rise up,
And challenges threaten,

Sing loudly
The songs of your souls,
The songs of the Infinite

With each other,
With the ancestors,
And with the earth, waters and sky.

These songs are here always
And they will guide us
As we go.

PRACTICE FOR THE WEEK

As We Go

We take our seats with awareness and bring ourselves to an awake and upright posture. Gently resting attention on the breath, we set the intention that each breath will bring soft, calming energy to and through us. Each breath is the song of the Infinite guiding our soul's journey.

After a few minutes, we say to ourselves this verse from Psalms:

I walk in the presence of the One in the lands of life.   Psalm 116:9

We repeat this phrase over and over, letting it travel with the breath. Each time we notice the attention has wandered, we give thanks for noticing and return the attention to the breath and the song of the psalmist:

I walk in the presence of the One in the lands of life.

We close the sit by declaring:
We walk together in the presence of the One in the lands of life.

Ha'azinu: Listen

Listen.
Remember.
Reflect on the paths that bought you to this moment.
Take notice of the twists and turns that have led you right here.

Lift up your face to receive blessings
That flow from the Mystery
And come down upon you like rain,
Blessings that come like soft showers,
Like dew upon the earth.   *Deuteronomy 32:2*

And notice the tendency to say
I don't deserve the blessings.
I have fallen short,
I have done wrong.

Notice the inclination to raise up misdeeds as barriers,
To use them as excuses
For not stepping forward into the fullness of life.

Listen and remember:
Life will continue to unfold with mystery, with passion, with grace.
Life will continue to be filled with joy, magnificence, disappointments
and pain.
You will love. You will dream. You will yearn. You will fly.
And you will fall.
You will get lost,
You will be dizzy with pain.
And I will be there with you, the Holy One declares,
Reminding you,
Again and again,
To listen, to remember,
And to return home to me.

Place these words upon your heart: *Deuteronomy 32:46*
    Everything that ever happened brought us to this moment
    And everything that will ever be flows forth from here.

And this is your life
Right here. Right now.   *Deuteronomy 32:47*

Lift your face to receive blessings,
Blessings that flow from the Infinite,
And come upon you like rain.

And place words upon your hearts
That will help you meet well
The offerings of each moment,
Words that will inspire you
To engage fully,
With this Mysterious Unfolding of Life.

PRACTICE FOR THE WEEK
Nishmat Chayim – The Breath of All Life

We take our seats with awareness and let our attention rest on the breath. We watch as the breath moves through the body and we feel the sensations in our chests, necks and shoulders. We feel the breath in our faces and down our arms. And we notice as the breath fills our stomachs and travels down our legs.

With gentle strength, we anchor our attention on the movement and sensations of the breath and we declare: *Nishmat Chayim*, the breath of all life flows through and within all. One breath flows through the trees, waters, all beings, all life. One breath flows through all.

With each breath we repeat, *Nishmat Chayim*, calling forth the awareness that there is one breath that flows through and fills all life.

Each time we notice that our attention has wandered, we give thanks for noticing and we do *teshuvah*: we return the attention to the present moment by noticing the sensations of the breath. Again and again, we return to the present. Again and again, we return to *Nishmat Chayim*, the breath of all life that flows through all.

150

We do this practice with compassion, remembering that every moment of distraction is an opportunity for *teshuvah*, for returning to the present.

As we close the sit, we give thanks for blessings in our lives. And we set an intention to remember that each in-breath is a gift and each out-breath an offering and there is one breath that flows through us all.

Hazak Hazak, V'nithazek.

May we go forward in strength.

May the words of our mouths, the intentions of our hearts And the work of our hands bring healing and love.

Infinite One, You have opened my understanding.
You have made it known to me that this is what you desire
For me to say:
Here I am, I have come with the scroll of the book
That is written upon me.
My deepest yearning is to live in alignment with the Highest Will,
To live the Torah that you placed within me.
And in gatherings large and small I will not be restrained.
I will speak for justice, faith, love and truth.

Psalm 40:7-11

Acknowledgements

This book was brought forth through the work of many hearts and hands.

To Carol Towarnicky, whose efforts, love and vision truly brought this book to be—gratitude beyond anything I could express. Carol's editing helped shape these words, her dedication and commitment fueled my strength and her companionship in this endeavor gave me courage and faith. I also think Carol read through this manuscript so many times, she might actually have parts of it memorized.

Much appreciation to Lance Laver and Phyllis Myers who read through this work with clear eyes and loving hearts. Gratitude to Bea Leopold who often weaves together projects underneath the surface.

So much gratitude to current and past *A Way In* board members: Lance Laver, Phyllis Myers, Lior Feldman, Rebecca Feldman, Stacey Meadows, Sharon Barr, Chris Taranta, Bea Leopold, Jane Weiss, Danielle Parmenter, Carol Towarnicky, Roz Katz and Pat Ryan. Their vision and dedication lift up and sustain *A Way In*. Their support and love makes possible the work I am blessed to do. Every day I am grateful for their partnership.

To the wide *A Way In* community, who travel with us online, come to our retreats, *daven* with us on Shabbat and holidays, thank you for calling forth the teachings. They only come through relationship.

To the Mishkan Shalom community, where I have served as rabbi for 25 years, a fountain of gratitude for all the ways you have encouraged my growth and inspired my exploration and discovery.

Much appreciation for the Institute for Jewish Spirituality, where I had the opportunity to develop these teachings as an online course. All I learned and discovered with IJS continues to grow and blossom within me.

To my teachers far and wide whose wisdom and insights are woven throughout my offerings, to my friends and family whose love lifts and holds me, to the red rock canyons of the southwest and to the trees, waters, birds, animals, plants and people of the Wissahickon, my home land, I bow in deep and abiding gratitude.

To the Mystery, the Source of All, may my appreciation be always, and may love and gratitude shape my words and deeds.

Rabbi Yael Levy

Rabbi Yael Levy's approach to Mindfulness is deeply rooted in Jewish tradition and is accessible to people of different faiths and paths. Her commitment to spiritual practice grows out of a passionate belief in its potential to change individuals and the world.

As rabbinic director of *A Way In* Jewish Mindfulness organization, Rabbi Levy leads contemplative retreats and Shabbat and holiday celebrations integrating Jewish practices and the wisdom of the earth. Her weekly meditations and teachings are shared internationally online and on social media.

Named as one of "America's Most Inspiring Rabbis" by the Jewish *Forward*, Rabbi Levy has been a scholar-in-residence in various settings throughout the country. She is a spiritual director to rabbinical students in the Reconstructionist and Reform movements and in private practice. Rabbi Levy leads Shabbat Mindfulness services twice a month at Mishkan Shalom synagogue in Philadelphia. She is a graduate of the Reconstructionist Rabbinical College and has trained with the Institute for Jewish Spirituality.

Rabbi Levy is the author of *Journey through the Wilderness: A Mindfulness Approach to the Ancient Jewish Practice of Counting the Omer; Chanukah Lights: Psalms for Hallel; Two Months of Adar: Time to Align.*

A Way In

Founded in 2009, *A Way In* is a Philadelphia-based organization that integrates Jewish wisdom with Mindfulness practices to direct the heart, awaken the attention and strengthen the capacity to meet well all that life brings. It is dedicated to being a source for healing, love and compassion.

A Way In offers retreats, weekly call-in Meditation Sits (live and recorded) as well as Shabbat and holiday services. Through its website, weekly newsletter and social media, *A Way In* provides Rabbi Yael Levy's teachings and suggestions for practice to an online community. Its resources are used in Jewish and non-Jewish settings, on wilderness retreats, with people serving time in prison and with children.

Find out more at:
Website: awayin.org
Instagram: @awayinorg
Facebook: facebook.com/jmindfulness
Twitter: @awayinorg

Made in the USA
Coppell, TX
19 March 2022

75256002R00095